VEGETARIAN PARIS

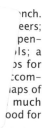

Paris has long been known ... world's gourmet dining epicer... not until now has the French been able to claim the ... "Veg-Friendly" bragging... Vegetarian Paris, the most ... hensive guide of its kind, ... more than 150 delectable destinations throughout the city's 20 unique arrondissements and arms readers with the information they need to eat well and have fun on their French sojourns.

...nch. ...eers; ...pen- ...ls; a ...s for ...com- ...aps of ... much ...ood for herbivores!

What's inside: All the delicious details on dozens of hot new veg restaurants, as well as tried-and-true favorites that range from macrobiotic and

About the author

Paris local and longtime vegan Aurelia d'Andrea has spent the better part of four years getting intimately acquainted with the City of Light's plant-based dining possibilities. Armed with a journalism degree and a hearty appetite, she's unearthed the best South Indian dosas, savory Vietnamese crepes, French mushroom pâtés, and buttery vegan croissants, and shares the details in this book on where to try them on your next trip to Paris.

Aurelia is the former editorial director of America's biggest selling vegan lifestyle magazine *VegNews*. Her other books include *Moon Living Abroad in France* and *Moon MapGuide Paris*. Her latest project is

www.swellmagazine.com

Sophia Pagan Photography

www.aureliadandrea.com

Vegetarian Paris, 1st edition
by Aurelia d'Andrea
ISBN 978-1-902259-18-5
www.vegetarianparis.com

Published August 2014 by
Vegetarian Guides Ltd, PO Box
2284, London W1A 5UH, England

Book layout designed by Irene
Schneider design.irene@gmail.com

Map data © OpenStreetMap
contributors, CC-BY-SA 2.0. Map
programming by Monika Szczerba.

Veggie Guides logo design Marion
Gillet www.mariongillet.com

Disributed in France, Belgium,
Switzerland and Quebec by Pollen
www.pollen-diffusion.com

Distributed in USA and Canada by
Book Publishing Company, TN
www.bookpubco.com

Distributed in UK and Ireland by
Gardners, Bertram, Bookspeed

Sales enquiries:
www.vegetarianguides.co.uk
sales@vegetarianguides.co.uk
Tel +44-20-3239 8433 (24 hours)
skype veggie_guides

Printed and bound by Bell & Bain,
Glasgow. www.bell-bain.com

If you want to review and
recommend this book with a
link to us, we will happily pay
you commission, see www.
vegetarianguides.co.uk/affiliate

Join the team: If you have updates,
or a group, shop or cafe and want
copies to resell or give as gifts,
we will do you a very attractive
discount. Contact updates@ or
sales@vegetarianguides.co.uk

Disclaimer: Restaurants are
continually changing their prices,
owners and opening hours and
sometimes close for holidays.
Every effort has been made to
ensure accuracy in this book,
however it is impossible to account
for every detail and mistakes can
occur. Before making a special
journey, we recommend you call
ahead to check details.

VEGETARIAN PARIS

by Aurelia d'Andrea

 Vegetarian Guides

CONTENTS

VEGGIE RESTAURANTS

VEGAN

VEGETARIAN

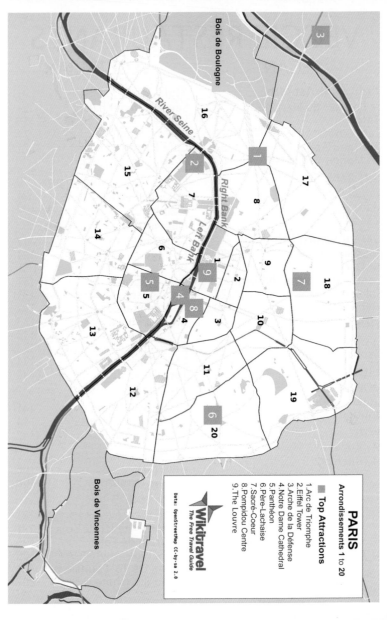

PARIS
Arrondissements 1 to 20

■ Top Attractions

1. Arc de Triomphe
2. Eiffel Tower
3. Arche de la Défense
4. Notre Dame Cathedral
5. Panthéon
6. Père-Lachaise
7. Sacré-Coeur
8. Pompidou Centre
9. The Louvre

Wikitravel
The Free Travel Guide

Data: OpenStreetMap CC-by-sa 2.0

Bois de Boulogne

Bois de Vincennes

River Seine

Right Bank

Left Bank

INTRODUCTION

Paris for vegetarians

Vegetarian Paris

Paris, France. Just whisper those two little words and a flash of vivid images spring to mind: The Eiffel Tower, *boulangeries* redolent with the yeasty aroma of warm baguettes, berets tilted at jaunty angles, sidewalk cafés. One of the last things anyone might think of when imagining the City of Light in all its glory is a café scene where meat and dairy are off the table, and in their place are flavorful, imaginative, locally grown, gorgeous foods. Well, such a thing does exist, though it is a relatively recent phenomenon.

Between 2012 and 2013, a half-dozen new veg restaurants opened their doors in Paris, and the trend is continuing on that upward swing, with several meat-free eateries launching in the French capital in 2014. Shifts are happening in the retail world, too, with more and more supermarkets carrying vegetarian specialty items including veggie burgers, non-dairy yogurts and milks, and other convenience foods. Supermarkets are also dedicating entire aisles to organic and gluten-free foods, hinting at a growing acceptance of "alternative" diets in a country with a very firm grip on its culinary traditions.

Each Parisian *arrondissement* has something to offer herbivores, from dairy-free ice-cream stands to meat-free burger bars. In this guide, you'll discover not only great vegetarian dining possibilities, but creative ideas on how to enjoy Paris's many attractions—museums, parks, monuments, shopping districts, architecture—while staying sated, hydrated, and entertained.

How To Use This Guide

This food, culture, and travel guide is not just for vegans and vegetarians, but also tourists with food sensitivities, environmentally conscious travelers, those interested in organic living, and globetrotters in search of a unique travel experience in what is, arguably, the world's most beautiful and romantic city.

To help you on your way, we've included a language primer to arm you with the most common culinary terms you'll encounter, and to encourage you to go local and impress the natives ("*s'il vous plaît*" and "*merci*" are *très important* and will take you very far).

Our Paris map introduces readers to the city's *arrondissements*, the 20 unique districts that spiral out like a snail's shell beginning at the Louvre

(1st) and ending in eastern Paris (20th), home to the famous Père Lachaise cemetery and some of the city's best music venues. The map also illustrates *Rive Gauche* and *Rive Droite* (left and right banks of the river Seine), and points out the major monuments and tourist sites for easy navigation.

Next, we introduce you to the wonderful vegan, vegetarian, and omnivorous restaurants, cafés, fast-food spots, boutiques, and other places that make the French capital such a welcoming place for herbivores. And in between, you'll meet some authentic Parisians who share their top tips for travelers, including their favorite local markets, dining spots, watering holes, wine shops, and day-trip destinations.

An important reminder while reading this guide is that wherever you are in Paris, you're rarely more than a 30-minute Métro ride to anywhere in the city, so you never have to feel resigned to eat *frites* and a salad at the corner brasserie. While this guide offers dining destinations in every *arrondissement*, you'll notice some corners of Paris are more bountiful in terms of edible possibilities than others. But don't forget the 30-minute rule and you'll never go hungry or settle for a substandard meal.

Understanding French Dining Hours

In Paris, and throughout the rest of France, there are three kinds

of dining hours: Standard, *service continu,* and *le snack* hours. Standard hours for lunch are 12.00-15.00. Evening meal hours are generally 19.00-22.00, and sometimes later. Breakfast isn't really a "thing" here; generally it's a grab-and-go croissant or a thimbleful of coffee at the corner café. Weekend brunch, however, is a recent phenomenon that's beginning to catch fire, so if you're hankering for a hearty morning meal, seek it out on Saturdays and Sundays beginning at about 11.00.

Some restaurants, however, offer all-day dining service known as *service continu* where you could order off the standard lunch menu at 16.00 or even 17.00 if you feel like it. Generally, brasseries and chain restaurants catering to tourists are the ones providing these off-hours opportunities. A third possibility is *le snack*: some cafés offer simple sandwiches or a very limited menu between standard meal times; look for an *ardoise* (chalkboard) advertising light bites that might include panini or salads.

If you're traveling with children, keep in mind that booster seats and high chairs aren't typically found in French restaurants. Infants are frequently left sleeping in their *poussettes* (strollers) while their parents eat, or, as is often the case, left at home.

And remember: Leaving a tip is optional!

Getting to Paris

and getting around by métro, bus, car, and bike

There are many means of getting to *la Ville Lumière* from wherever you are in the world, including planes, trains, buses, and boats. Once you're here, you'll discover excellent public-transit options including the ride-share system called *co-voiturage* that allows you to share expenses, meet new people, and get where you need to go even when the country is in the throes of a pesky transportation *grève* (strike).

Charles De Gaulle International Airport

Most international flights land at Charles de Gaulle, which the French refer to as "Roissy." To get to Paris from the airport, there are several options including the cheap (€9.50) RER B train. Leaving from Terminal 2, it takes about 30 minutes to get to Gare du Nord. (If your flight arrives at Terminal 1, there's a free shuttle bus to Terminal 2.) Tickets can be purchased from kiosks in the station or from a vendor inside one of the station ticket booths.

Another option is Roissybus (€10), which circles each terminal every 15 minutes from 05:45-20.00, every 20 minutes between 20.00-22.00, and every 30 minutes between 22.00-23.00. Your bus will deposit you in central Paris behind the Opéra Garnier. The trip runs about 45-60 minutes. Tickets can be purchased on board.

Air France buses are big and cushy, and leave from Terminal 1 and 2 every 15 minutes from 05.45 to 23.00, with stops at Porte Maillot and Place de l'Étoile (the Arc de Triomphe). Tickets cost €16.10 and the trip takes about an hour. Going the opposite direction, buses also leave from Gare de Lyon and Montparnasse station. Tickets can be purchased on board the bus.

The least expensive option is Bus 350, which runs from the airport train station to Gare du Nord every 15 minutes Monday through Friday, and every half-hour on weekends. The trip takes about 45-60 minutes, and you can purchase tickets (€5.65) from the driver.

Arriving By Train

Paris's six main train stations each offer service to different regions in France and other countries. At Gare d'Austerlitz (in the 13th arrondissement) you can catch trains to southwest France, Spain, and Portugal; at Gare de l'Est (10th), you'll be able to reach eastern France and Germany; trains departing Gare de Lyon (12th) head to southern and eastern France, Switzerland, and

Italy; Gare Montparnasse(15th) serves Brittany and Bordeaux; Gare Saint-Lazare (9th) trains depart for Normandy; and trains from Gare du Nord (10th) leave for Belgium, Holland, Germany, and England.

At each station you'll find both *grande ligne* TGV trains for long-distance trips and TER suburban lines for shorter trips. To scout ticket prices online, visit www.sncf.com. Don't forget to *composter* (punch) your ticket in one of the yellow machines on the platform before you board the train. If you haven't enough time, present yourself to a conductor as soon as you board the train so you aren't charged a cheater's fine.

Public Transportation

Paris has an extraordinary public transportation system. Métro lines link the entire city and close suburbs and run between 05:30-01.00 weekly, and until 02:15 Fridays and Saturdays. The same type of ticket you use for the Métro can be used for buses and trams. Tickets can be purchased from kiosks or human-staffed booths in the station, either as individual tickets or as a *carnet*, or bundle of 10 tickets. This is the less-expensive option; when purchased individually, each ticket costs €1.70, but when bought in lots of 10, the price drops to €1.37 each. The prices increase every year, but tickets never expire, so you can use the tickets you bought ten years ago on the train today if you've got them!

As long as you don't exit the station, you can use a single Métro ticket to transfer as many times as needed to reach your final destination. Hold onto your ticket, though; inspections are relatively common and you could be ticketed for not having proof you paid. To transfer between buses or trams you must use a second ticket.

If you miss the last Métro, you can catch the Noctilien night bus (www. noctilien.fr), which runs 01:00-05:30 nightly. Buses depart from Châtelet, Montparnasse, and Gare du Nord, and travel the main thoroughfares within the city and into the suburbs. One bus per Noctilien line runs every hour. A Métro ticket also allows you to ride on the RER suburban trains within Paris city limits. To view Métro, bus, tramway, or RER itineraries, visit www. vianavigo.fr.

Co-Voiturage

Several ride-sharing organizaitons exist in France, but Co-Voiturage (www.covoiturage.fr) is the most popular. Sign up for free online, then get in touch with the driver offering up seats in his or her car. Recent fares include €23 to Brussels, €35 to Bordeaux, and €45 to London. Each driver's profile includes details on such things as whether dogs or smoking is allowed in the vehicle, whether they're chatty, or if they prefer to listen to music instead of your mediocre French. Drivers are also rated by previous passengers on their driving, timeliness, and friendliness.

Public Bike Share

Vélib' (www.velib.paris.fr), a city-sponsored bicycle-hire service, allows anyone over the age of 14 to rent a bicycle from one of nearly 2,000 terminals throughout Paris and the close suburbs, and to conveniently drop your bike off at any station when you're ready. Customers have the option to apply for a year's subscription (€19-39, depending on the type of subscription) or a short-term *abonnement*. Make sure your bank or credit card has a microchip that meets EMV standards. Don't have a card with a *puce*? Rent online and bypass that problem! A short-term subscription costs €1.70 for one day and €8 for seven days. This allows you to take the bicycle for free for the first half-hour, but costs €1 for the second half hour, €2 for the following half hour, and €4 for the third half hour. A deposit of €150 is pre-authorized from your card, but not withdrawn. When returning

your bike to the terminal, ensure it is properly attached, and that the green "locked" light is indicated. Also keep all receipts, should you need to make any claims.

Autolib'

The newest public transportation system to hit Paris is the car-share program called Autolib'. Subscribing online (www.autolib.eu) for periods of a day, week, month, or year gives you access to a fleet of four-seat electric "Bluecars" stationed throughout Paris and the Île-de-France region. A valid driver's license and international permit are required for non-EU drivers, and charges average €10 to €14 per hour. This option is best for short, one-way trips.

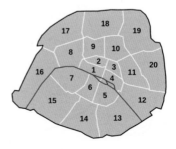

Paris Accommodation

At Home in the City of Light

So you haven't scored your Parisian pied-a-terre—yet. Until you find that perfect, permanent foothold here, you'll need a temporary place to stay, right? Options abound, from camping grounds to rooms in private homes, to hostels and five-star hotels. Unlike London and some other major metropolises, Paris is an affordable hotel center, and generally, a couple can find a private room in a clean, comfy hotel for the same price you'd pay for two people at a hostel. Ever since the Gentle Gourmet B&B closed its doors (to focus on the vegan Gentle Gourmet café), there's been a big void in the veg-friendly accommodations market, but here are a few options to kick start your search. Before settling on any one place, be sure to check TripAdvisor to avoid any unfortunate surprises.

TIP: In Paris zipcodes 75001 to 75020, the number of the arrondissement is indicated by the last two digits.

Air bnb
Rooms in private homes

➤ www.airbnb.com

Finding a private room in a vegetarian household is easy with Airbnb's search filter. Just type "vegetarian" into the Keywords filter, and choose among dozens of possibilities in every neighwborhood and price range.

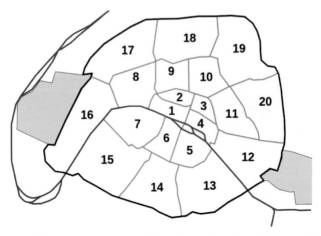

Chain Hotels/Motels

Accor Hotel Group
Hotel chain

↖ www.accorhotels.com

From bare bones, dormitory-style (yet still private) rooms at rock-bottom prices to deluxe rooms with every variety of mod-con, you'll find something to fit your budget within the Accor Hotel group. Rates begin at €39 at the two Paris locations of Formule 1 (Porte de Montmartre and Porte de Châtillon), which are intended for road travelers and found just off the Périphérique motorway that rings Paris. For something a bit more upscale, try a Mercure or Novotel. New under the Accor Hotel umbrella is Ibis (see below) and Ibis Styles.

Ibis
Hotel chain

↖ www.ibis.com

The Ibis chain has expanded to include Ibis Styles—smart, business-style accommodations with free wifi and breakfast (BYOSM—Bring Your Own Soy Milk) included. Room rates begin at €61 at several locations throughout Paris, including Montmartre and République, and if you tick the boxes for the Fl and Formule 1 hotels, you'll find even more affordable rooms just outside the Périphérique.

Timhotel
Hotel chain

↖ www.timhotel.com

With several locations in Paris, this chain offers predictable comfort and style, free wifi, and tea/coffee makers in the rooms. Rates begin at around €70. Basic and clean.

Independent Accommodation

10th

Chambres de la Grande Porte
Vegetarian bed & breakfast

☛ 10 rue des Petites Ecuries
   Cross street: rue du Faubourg Saint-Denis
☎ 06 63 42 35 32
⊖ Métro: Chateau d'Eau
↖ www.chambresdelagrandeporte.fr

Rates at this vegetarian—yes, vegetarian!—B&B begin at €78 (low season rate). The hosts happily accommodate vegans, and dinner is also an option. The four guest rooms have showers, but toilets are shared. Also three apartments at the same location. The neighborhood is interesting, with lots of bars and proximity to veg-friendly restaurants, including Asian-vegetarian hotspot Végébowl (see pg. 117). English spoken.

12th

Hotel Mistral
Independent hotel

- 📍 3 Rue Chaligny
  Cross street: rue Diderot
- 📞 01 46 28 10 20
- 🚇 Métro: Reuilly–Diderot
- 🔗 www.hotelparismistral.com

Rooms start at €59 at this cute little hotel on a calm street in eastern Paris. Walking distance to the Gentle Gourmet and other Bastille-area veg restaurants, and just five minutes from Gare de Lyon and the bustling Marché d'Aligre.

18th

Parisian Days
Private residence

- 📍 on rue Caulaincourt
  Cross street: Lamarck
- 🚇 Métro: Lamarck-Caulaincourt
- 🔗 www.parisiandays.com
  paul@parisiandays.com

Rent a bright, airy studio apartment from Paul, your friendly, bilingual host. The Montmartre neighborhood is quintessentially Parisian (read: lined with cafes and beautiful old trees). Paul also offers local tours that include jaunts to off-the-beaten-path neighborhoods.

20th

Mama Shelter
Independent hotel

- 📍 109 rue de Bagnolet
  Cross street: rue des Pyrénées
- 📞 01 43 48 48 48
- 🚇 Métro: Alexandre Dumas or
  Porte de Bagnolet
- 🔗 www.mamashelter.com

Rates begin at €79 at this chic, Philippe Starck-designed hotel on the edge of eastern Paris. The on-site pizza restaurant (pg.210) is vegan-friendly, and the neighborhood offers an interesting demographic mix of old and new. Indie music venue Flèche d'Or is just across the street.

Boulogne–Billancourt

Chez Emoke
Room in private house

- 📍 21 quai Alphonse le Gallo
  Cross street: rue Gallieni
  (see map 16th, p.179)
- 📞 01 41 31 01 49
- 🚇 Métro: Pont de Sèvres

In a quiet, Seine-side neighborhood just over the Périphérique in southern Paris, a vivacious Hungarian expat offers simple, private accommodations in her bright, modern apartment. The price is right at €40/55 (single/double), breakfast included. Let her know if you're vegan! Nature lovers will appreciate the easy access to the beautiful Parc de Saint-Cloud just across the river.

Home Away from Home

How-to tips from a short-term rental specialist

Vegans and vegetarians, more than any other category of traveler, can really benefit from a vacation apartment rental. The luxury of a kitchen allows you to take advantage of Paris's amazing outdoor markets brimming with fresh produce, and to prepare meat-free meals at home. And having a refrigerator at your disposal means cold soymilk and muesli is *always* on the morning menu. So, where does one begin when looking for a rental?

Gail Boisclair is here to help. She's the owner of PerfectlyParis (www.perfectlyparis.info, also free apps for iPhone and Android), a company offering short-term Paris apartment rentals, specialising in Montmartre and surrounding neighborhoods. *Condé Nast Traveler* has named her their Top Villa Rental Specialist for Paris every year since 2008. These are her top tips for veggie visitors seeking a home away from home in the City of Light.

#1 Paris is a year-round destination, so **book early – start looking at least 6 months in advance for your best choice**. Other than January through March, November, and early December, finding something at the last minute can be very difficult.

#2 Size-wise, Paris is a small city with a very efficient transit system, so **location may not be as important as you think**. Pick a flat you would look forward to going home to at the end of your day and make sure it is close to a métro station.

#3 Ask the owner or rental agency for a list of nearby grocery stores, outdoor markets, and boulangeries. Apartments have the advantage of kitchens, so **consider proximity to food shops where you can buy fresh produce** to prepare veg meals. Eating one or two meals at home is a great money-saver, too.

#4 **Avoid scams**! Do NOT book if you are asked to pay by Western Union, MoneyGram, etc.) and confirm in advance that the agency you are renting from is reputable. Do searches on the internet and in travel forums to find out what people have to say about the company.

#5 Learn what to do in an emergency. **Ask for a local contact** in case something goes wrong or you need help.

Keep in mind that renting an apartment is not for everyone. Apartments have their own personalities and quirks – the 100-year-old parquet floors may creak, and there won't be a front desk or concierge at your disposal. If you are a traveler who relies on them, a hotel may be a better alternative for you (although it would not have the same charm and you would not feel that you are living like a Parisian!).

My Favorite Veg Table

V-Listers reveal their favorite Paris dining spots

Dynise Balcavage

▶ www.urbanvegan.net

Dynise, whose love affair with Paris began in high school, lives in Philadelphia, but visits the French capital regularly—twice as a as a special guest speaker at Paris Vegan Day. Her latest cookbook, *Pies and Tarts with Heart*, has already got mouths salivating from Canada to the Côte d'Azur.

My favorite veg table in Paris is **Loving Hut** *(11th, pg. 145). Cities all over the world house their own Loving Huts;*

they border on being vegan clichés and vary in quality from "meh" to "oh là là!" Paris's Loving Hut definitely falls into the latter category. I especially adore their potage au potiron (pumpkin soup) – so comforting on a chilly autumn evening. Ultracreamy, made with a coconut base and fragrant, subtle spices, it warms you down to your soul. It tastes as if it came straight from grandma's kitchen. In the event that you are missing the taste of dairy cheese, the Loving Hut's vegan cheese board is frighteningly reminiscent of cow's cheese, and is reasonably priced. And if you are craving a well-made breakfast café au lait, this is also the place to go. Both its decor and service are sunny and cheerful.

David Ivar aka Yaya
Herman Dune/Black Yaya

▶ www.blackyaya.com

Black Yaya is the latest musical incarnation of Paris-based musician David Ivar. He regularly tours the world playing stadium-size music festivals and intimate venues alike. His newest single *Paint a Smile On Me* was released on Partyfine records in late 2013.

I'm vegan and my favorite veg tables in Paris are:

Loving Hut (11th, pg. 145) Entirely vegan. Delicious and great service.

L'As Du Fallafel (4th, pg. 85) The best falafel In the world, Holy Land Included.

Chez Taéko Traiteur japonais at the Marché des Enfants Rouges (3rd, pg. 32) The agedashi tofu is the only vegan dish offered,but it so good that it's worth it.

La Bricciola (14 rue Normandie, 3rd) The Marinara pizza is a great classic vegan option at this pizzeria with great service and awesome wine.

Flip Grater

▶ www.flipgrater.com

Kiwi musician Flip spends half the year writing, performing, and eating (and drinking) in Paris, and the other half doing same in her Antipodean hometown. Her latest book *The*

Cookbook Tour: Europe--Adventures in Food and Music is available through Bateman Publishing.

On a payday I love Septime (80 rue de Charonne, 11th). It's a wonderful fine Italian restaurant that does a vegetarian or vegan dégustation menu upon request—even without prior notice if you smile sweetly at the Italian waiters. Favourite dish: Braised white asparagus with crispy fried garlic flakes and coriander leaves.

On the cheaper end of the scale there's Rouleau de Printemps (20th, pg. 210), my favourite Vietnamese spot. It has about six crammed-in tables and is always hot and busy but it has a full vegetarian menu and the food is truly good. Favourite dish: rice noodle salad with fresh mint, carrot, lettuce and coriander with sweet soy dressing, sour chilli sauce and a cold beer.

Carole Raphaelle Davis

Carole is an animal-rights activist, vegan and the author of *The Diary of Jinky: Dog of a Hollywood Wife*. She divides her time between LA and Nice, France, where she performs, writes and cooks.

L'Arpège (7th, pg. 106) is THE place to dine veggie in Paris. Finally--haute cuisine that's ethical! Passard, the chef, is a genius. Being a French woman, I like dressing up and partici-pating in the aesthetic scene to match the elegance of the food. I hope l'Arpège opens the door for vegan haute cuisine in every city in France. Dining out doesn't get more refined than this. Passard lifts veganism to a level of high art in a uniquely French way and proves that French cuisine can be the best in the world without harming our friends, the animals.

Dan with Pink and Stella McCartney at Paris Fashion Week

photo Mary McCartney

Dan Mathews

▶ www.peta.org

Dan is more than just the Vice-President of People for the Ethical Treatment of Animals, he's also a talented writer whose laugh-out-loud funny autobiography, *Committed: A Rabble-Rouser's Memoir*, should be on every animal-lover's reading list.

Good food in Paris means a lot to me as I usually enjoy it after a day or two in jail following an exciting PETA protest. Parisian jails don't cater to vegans so when I'm set free I rush directly to **Le Potager du Marais** *(3rd, pg. 70). The celery root bisque is magnifique, as is the seitan with mushroom-cognac sauce, even though I don't usually like mushrooms.*

This candlelit hotspot has special meaning because it is where John Galliano invited me to dinner to say that part of his rehab involved working with animals to learn empathy, and as part of his sobriety he started eating vegan. This former PETA target is now a friend. Now, instead of going to jail after disrupting a Galliano fur and leather show, the two of us talk animal rights over a gourmet vegan dinner.

COMMITTED

"SMART, SILLY, and DOWNRIGHT READABLE, WITH UNFLAPPABLE SPIRIT, LIKE DAVID SEDARIS BUT WITH A MISSION." —LEZ GESTWICKI

A RABBLE-ROUSER'S MEMOIR

DAN MATHEWS

Adam Turner aka Beat Assailant

▸ Twitter.com/beatassailant
Facebook.com//pages/Beat-
Assailant/54837965443

Paris-based hip-hop artist Beat Assailant has been making dance-worthy, jazz-influenced music for more than a decade, and continues to dazzle audiences around the world with his energetic live performances. His fifth studio album *City Never Sleeps* was released in May 2014.

It was difficult for me to choose my favorite veggie spot in Paris and that's proof that the City of Light has come a long way. When I first moved to Paris over 10 years ago, I had to cook almost all of my meals at home. Never in my wildest dreams did I think there would ever be a place like **East Side Burgers** *(11th, pg. 141) in Paris. With a rotating menu that offers two different burger choices*

daily, fries to die for, vegan hot dogs, nuggets, and even vegan desserts, this 100-percent vegetarian fast food restaurant is a must visit! Every-thing's great here, but I always order the "Forestier" burger with lettuce, mushroom-tofu steak, caramelized onions, and tomato. And don't forget to order an extra side of fries. I think I already mentioned they're to die for!

photo by Cody Clarke

Ana Homayoun

www.anahomayoun.com

Ana, a San Francisco-based educator, lifestyle coach, vegan, and author, began traveling regularly to Paris after college and returns for fun and inspiration. Her latest book, *The Myth of The Perfect Girl: Helping Our Daughters Find Authentic Success and Happiness in School and Life*, has been hailed by teen girls and moms alike.

When I am in Paris, I generally stay in an apartment in Le Marais. I spend the early morning hours writing at my kitchen table and then head over to Rose Bakery for lunch (3rd, pg. 74).

Though there are several locations throughout the city, I love the spot in the Marais the best. The interior is casual and unpretentious, and those who sit in the front room can watch the baked goods being created right before their eyes.

Although Rose Bakery isn't strictly vegan, they offer quite a few vegan,

gluten-free and organic options. I typically order the assorted salad plate of the day, and simply ask them to make sure to only include vegan salads on my plate (there are usually quite a few delicious choices). Sometimes, I also treat myself to the vegan soup option, and a pot of green tea.

They also have organic produce available for purchase, so in the summer I usually pick up a melon or some peaches for later in the day.

One of my favorite side notes: the tables are lined with butcher block paper, and more than once I've used the paper to start outlining a new writing idea that spontaneously came to me in the middle of lunch.

Helping Our Daughters Find Authentic Success and Happiness in School and Life

"Ana Homayoun shows what parents and educators can do to help girls navigate these turbulent years with confidence and purpose."
–Michael Gurian, author of *The Wonder of Girls*

The Myth of the Perfect Girl

Ana Homayoun
Author of
That Crumpled Paper Was Due Last Week

Mark Hawthorne

▸ www.markhawthorne.com

Mark loves the adventure of travel. He is the author of *Bleating Hearts: The Hidden World of Animal Suffering* and *Striking at the Roots: A Practical Guide to Animal Activism*. You'll find him tweeting @markhawthorne.

If there's one thing I appreciate while traveling it's finding delicious vegan food, so I was delighted when my wife and I discovered the **Gentle Gourmet Cafe** *(12th, pg. 152) near la Bastille. The atmosphere may be upscale, but the staff is friendly, efficient, and amiably bilingual. A cozy indoor/outdoor area makes for splendid sidewalk dining no matter what the weather. Couple this with the cafe's extensive menu and you've got the perfect place to linger over breakfast, lunch, or dinner while watching the city go by. I'm particularly fond of the baguette brimming with vegan ham and cheese. Do save room for dessert—you will not be disappointed when you tuck into some of the most mouthwatering sweets Paris has to offer.*

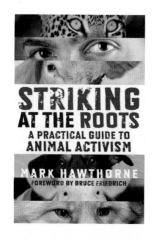

Parisian Food Landscape

Navigating the Cornucopia of Dining Options

The café still rules the French dining scene, but there are other options. Seek out these dining possibilities when a veg restaurant isn't an option.

Chinois (Chinese) Traiteurs

These Asian delicatessens are ubiquitous in big cities and bigger towns throughout France, and usually offer at least one or two cheap, filling, vegan options. Most all are set up the same way: long glass counter full of pre-cooked Asian plates, which are microwaved before serving. Look for *nem aux legumes* (vegetable spring rolls), *nouilles aux legumes* (noodles with vegetables), and stir-fried vegetables with rice. Desserts like *perles de coco* are more often than not vegan. Wine is also generally served here. Expect to be asked "Pour emporter?" which means "To go?" If you want to dine in, say "pour ici" (for here).

French Brasseries

This is the most typical kind of restaurant you'll find in France, and for a long time, they were veritable wastelands for vegetarians and especially vegans. Today, you'll always be able to find at least a salad, bread, and fries to make a meal out of, and sometimes they'll surprise you by offering a pasta dish that's vegan. Look for *salade composée* (where ingredients are arranged beautifully on a plate rather than mixed together), and if you don't see one marked "vegetarian," ask if they can make you one *sans oeuf* (without egg), *sans fromage* (without cheese), and *sans viande* (without meat). Creamy-looking salad dressings are often (surprisingly) dairy-free and made from emulsified mustard, oil, and vinegar, but to play it safe, you may want to ask for *huile et vinaigre* (oil and vinegar).

Indian/Sri Lankan

You'll find south Asian eateries throughout France, but these can be a little trickier for vegans since milk products are generally an integral part of the cuisine. Steer away from naan, which is often made with milk, and stick with other breads like chapati or paratha. Dishes typically made without dairy include *aloo gobi* (potato and cauliflower curry) and *benghan bartha* (eggplant). South Indian and Sri Lankan restaurants generally offer good snacking opportunities, with treats like *bonda* (battered and fried potato balls), *vada* (savory donuts), and *dosas* (thin crepes). Fortunately, you'll find Indians are likely bilingual in English, which makes choosing meat- and dairy-free meals easier.

Italian

Italian restaurants will become your go-to favorites for reliable sources of veg meals. Vegans can ask for your vegetarian pizza sans fromage, and pair it with an insalata mista (mixed-greens salad) and a pichet of Italian wine for a filling, tasty meal. Pasta dishes that are typically vegetarian include pasta aglio e olio (garlic and olive oil) or pomodoro (tomato and garlic). The odds are good that the lemon sorbet is vegan, too. To mimic the fatty richness of cheese, you might ask for "huile pimentée" to drizzle over your pie or pasta.

Japonais (Japanese)

Japanese restaurants are becoming increasingly popular throughout France, and offer some interesting dining possibilities for vegans. Generally, miso soup is made with dashi, a fish stock, but *salad d'algue* (seaweed salad), *salad de choux* (marinated cabbage salad) *maki de concombre* (cucumber rolls), and *maki d'avocat* (avocado rolls) are made without fish. Note that a recent phenomenon in French-made Japanese cuisine is the addition of cheese to sushi rolls. Really. French chains with vegetarian options include Sushi Shop and Planet Sushi.

Libanais (Lebanese)

These ubiquitous establishments usually have a fast-food vibe, and prices to match. At Lebanese restaurants, you'll always have the possibility of eating falafel, or a vegetable plate (plat végétarien) that generally includes hummus, stuffed vine leaves, tabouli salad, and pita bread. Watch out for some of the olive-based spreads, which sometimes contain anchovy. Spinach pies are generally vegan. Ask!

North African (Moroccan, Tunisian, and Algerian)

Traditional couscous végétarien and tajine végétarien are easy-to-find options, and at North African bakeries, a delicious snack called m'semmen—a semolina crepe stuffed with tomatoes and peppers, with a spicy kick—is a tasty vegan option. Kesra, an unleavened semolina galette—is another tasty treat to try. Brik is a phyllo-style pastry sometimes served stuffed with vegetables.

In-a-Pinch
Restaurant Chains

You're starving, can't find a map, and if you don't eat tout de suite, your blood sugar will plummet to bad-mood-inducing levels. Stop, take a look around, and see if you can spot any one of these restaurant chains sprinkled throughout Paris that offer at least one or two substantial veg dishes.

Cojean
k www.cojean.fr

Salads, wheat grass juice, and other freshly prepared items served in a modern, fast-casual environment. Soups are vegan, and include crazy concoctions like wasabi-pea. More than a dozen locations throughout Paris, most clustered in the 8th arrondissement, but also near the organic Raspail market (in the 6th) and near the Louvre.

Indiana Café
k www.indianacafe.fr

This TexMex chain offers more than a dozen locations scattered throughout Paris in prime shopping/sightseeing hubs including Pigalle (near the Moulin Rouge), République, and Denfert-Rochereau (if you're headed to the Catacombs). Unlike many chains, they're open every day and offer *service continu* dining service. Look for the vegetarian section of the menu, and vegans should ask for anything that looks interesting to be made "*sans fromage*." ("without cheese")

Le Pain Quotidien
k www.lepainquotidien.fr

Choose among gorgeous salads, soups, and breads that form a filling, hearty meal. Vegetarian dishes marked with a (V), and most are already vegan or can be made vegan. Nice atmosphere, with communal tables and a rustic vibe.

Le Paradis du Fruit
k www.leparadisdufruit.fr

A pleasant place to eat if you want something light and want to enjoy it while sitting in a chic, touristy environment. A few vegan options include quinoa and vegetables, gazpacho, and soymilk smoothies. Cocktails, beer and wine served, too. A dozen locations throughout Paris, including near the Champs Elysées, Les Halles, and Montparnasse.

Exki

▸ www.exki.fr

You'll always find a vegan soup of the day, served with delicious whole-meal bread (or more pedestrian white if you prefer), plus a variety of salads, sandwiches, and drinks that are suitable for vegans.

Starbucks

▸ www.starbucks.fr

If you can't live without your morning or afternoon pick-me-up, Starbucks offers soy lattes at around 40 locations throughout Paris, including rue de Rivoli (several locations), the Champs Elysées, Pigalle, and Gare Saint-Lazare.

Subway

▸ www.subwayfrance.fr

There are more than 60 of these fast-food sandwich shops scattered throughout the French capital, and they're easy to find if you follow the distinct scent of baking bread to the nearest green storefront. All outlets offer a vegan option with vegetables on Italian-style bread, and many offer a vegetarian "steak" that can be turned into a sandwich or a salad topping.

Cooking at Your Home Away from Home
Supermarkets

Instead of staying in a hotel where you're obligated to dine out, consider renting an apartment for your stay. This option gives you the flexibility to prepare meals in your own kitchen, and experience the fun of shopping at French markets and preparing vegan meals you know are healthy, wholesome, and 100 percent meat-free. Once you've shopped for fresh produce at one of Paris's many outdoor markets (nearly all are closed Mondays), stop into these shops to gather the rest of the ingredients you'll need to make a fabulously memorable meal.

Picard

The space-age frozen-food store chain found throughout France, offers a surprising number of veg possibilities for those with the means to store and prepare them (French refrigerators are notoriously small, and freezers are even smaller). Photos and prices are displayed above the item stored below in sliding-glass-door freezers.

Sorbets—The pineapple-passionfruit sorbet by Bonne Maman is particularly good.

Galettes de blé noir—To make traditional savory Breton crepes at home, stuff with avocado, vegan cheese, and sautéed mushrooms.

Bhajis and pakoras—In case you're too tired to head to the 10th for the fresh stuff.

Vietnamese nems (fried eggless eggrolls)—for making that classic rice-noodle salad called *bo bun* on the fly.

Sticky rice with coconut—because, why not?

Monoprix and Monop'

Shop this ubiquitous chain department store/grocery store for its house-brand smoked or herbed tofu (look for it in the refrigerator section in a bright yellow package), grain-based "steaks," vegan pâtés (in the "bio" aisle), rice cakes, vegan dark chocolate bars, and prefab salads (carrot, beet, tabouli) and other prepared dishes.

Carrefour

One of France's big grocery store chains is a treasure trove of "bio" (organic) goodies and accidentally vegan treats, like soymilk and other non-dairy milks, hummus, Speculoos cookies and spread, and GMO-free Sojasun brand products like yogurt, pudding, faux ground beef, and others.

Franprix

Another ubiquitous chain of small grocery stores where you can procure necessities like olives, chips, organic wines, canned beans, quinoa (in the "bio" section), and other veg comestibles. Look for dairy-free yogurts and puddings in the dairy case, and a variety of ready-made salads in the refrigerator section.

Natural Food Chains

Health food and wholefood chain stores

This selection of natural food stores will help you get prepared for your next picnic or make-it-at-home meal. The addresses listed are those closest to major tourist attractions, and appear on the arrondissement maps in this book, but don't represent the full scope of possibilities available in the city. Independent stores are listed in the restaurant section.

Bio c'Bon

This newest organic chain to hit the scene has a growing number of outlets throughout Paris. Look for the big green-and-yellow sign, and pop in for a good selection of bulk items, organic fruit, prefab salads, fake meats, and gluten-free items. Bonus! Open on Sundays until 13.00.

- 9 place Pigalle, 9th (Montmarte/ Moulin Rouge)
- 26 rue du Renard, 4th (Centre Georges Pompidou)
- www.bio-c-bon.eu

Biocoop/Le Retour à la Terre

These are true cooperatives with an old-school natural-food-store vibe, which makes sense when you consider they've been around for more than 25 years. Here, you'll discover lots of bulk items, personal-care products, an organic deli case, a bakery section, and fresh produce. Also offers a good section of household items, in case you need to source that all-important corkscrew or can opener.

- 44 blvd de Grenelle, 15th (Eiffel Tower)
- 1 rue le Goff/12 rue Malebranche, 5th (Luxembourg Gardens)
- www.biocoop.fr

Naturalia

The most ubiquitous chain, you'll find this natural food giant in nearly every arrondissement, sometimes with multiple locations. You want it? They've got it, from chestnut milk and vegetarian dog food to smoked tempeh and agave nectar. Vitamins, personal-care products, fresh produce, and fresh-baked breads are available in every store.

- 84 rue Beaubourg, 3rd (Centre Georges Pompidou, Musée des Arts et Métiers)
- 94 rue Mouffetard, 5th (rue Mouffetard shopping district)
- 38 ave de la Motte-Picquet, 7th (Eiffel Tower)
- www.naturalia.fr

Les Nouveaux Robinson/ Bio Génération

The first organic market in the Paris region has expanded into a mini-empire of cooperative markets called either Les Nouveaux Robinson or Bio Generation (the former is in the process of acquiring the latter). Vitamins, dried fruit, breads, and vegan dairy products are some of the items you might find at one of these friendly stores.

- 68–70 rue du Cherche-Midi, 6th (Luxembourg Gardens)
- 78 boulevard Saint Michel, 6th (Luxembourg Gardens/Latin Quarter)
- 34 rue d'Aligre, 12th (Marché d'Aligre)
- www.nouveauxrobinson.fr

La Vie Claire

One of the last independent natural food chains in Paris (Naturalia is buying them all up), this is a good spot to stock up on smoked tempeh and healthy picnic items. On-site naturopaths to help you with your health-related questions, and both shops listed below have deli counters where you can procure salads, sandwiches, and quiches to go.

- 85 blvd Haussmann, 8th (Printemps and Galleries Lafayette)
- 76–80 rue Saint-Honoré, 1st (Louvre/Les Halles)
- www.lavieclaire.com

Paris Paysanne's quick & dirty guide to

Paris Markets

by Emily Dilling Poulain

photo by Kristen Beddard

Whenever I visit a new city, one of my first stops is the local market. These hubs of activity offer insight into the culture and kitchens of the city you are visiting. Unlike typical tourist destinations, open-air markets provide an authentic opportunity to see how locals live and participate in the excitement of both the everyday and extraordinary experience of buying food.

Paris markets are perfect places to check out seasonal produce, grab a quick snack, or stock up on everything you need to make a great vegetarian meal. Since 2010, my website Paris Paysanne (www.parispaysanne.com) has provided guidance on where to

find the best in locally grown and independently produced fruits and vegetables at Paris markets. Whether you're a fan of all-organic, super-local, or uncommon vegetable varieties, Paris has just the market for you. Here are a few of my favorite spots to shop:

Marché couvert des Enfants Rouges
3rd arrondissement indoor market

- 39 rue de Bretagne, 75003
- Métro: Filles du Calvaire
- Tu–W 9.00–20.00, Th–Sa 9:00–23.00, Su 9.00–15.00

Many of Paris's covered markets seem to have lost their luster or fallen into a state of disuse. Luckily this is not

the case with the *Marché des Enfants Rouges* where you will find aisles lined with lunch counters offering organic and vegetarian meal options. Visit the friendly Alain and have him prepare the southern specialty *socca*, a chickpea-based crêpe that is both vegan and gluten free and absolutely delicious when topped with some fresh ground pepper.

Marché Saxe-Breteuil
7th arrondissement street market

- 🠖 avenue de Saxe, 75007
- ⊖ Métro: Ségur
- ◑ Th 07.00-14.30 and Sa 07.00-15.00

Located in the shadow of the Eiffel Tower, this postcard-perfect market is well worth checking out. Independent farmers come out to sell freshly picked produce on the weekend. I always visit the Le Trepied stand for a large selection of heirloom varieties that change with the season. The vendors here are friendly and always ready to share suggestions for simple vegetarian recipes.

Marché Cours de Vincennes
12th arrondissement street market

- 🠖 cours de Vincennes- in between bd. Picpus and rue Arnold Netter
- ⊖ Métro: Picpus
- ◑ W 07.00-14.30 and Sa 07.00-15.00

While it may be a bit off the beaten path, Marché Cours de Vincennes deserves a visit if you're a hardcore locavore. Here you will find a half-

dozen vendors from the Île-de-France region. At these stands, you will find produce that was harvested that morning and travelled less than 25 miles to make it to the market.

Marché Biologique des Batignolles
17th arrondissement street market

- 🠖 34 boulevard des Batignolles
- ⊖ Métro: Place de Clichy or Rome
- ◑ Saturdays 08.00-13.30

This market is one of the three organic markets in Paris. All the vendors here are certified organic, and a handful of them have farms near Paris. Be sure to stop by Hermione Boehrer's stand for a wheatgrass shot, then sniff out a vegan, gluten-free chickpea *galette* served fresh off the griddle.

Marché couvert Batignolles
17th arrondissement indoor market

- 🠖 96 bis rue Lemercier, 75017
- ⊖ Métro: Brochant
- ◑ Tu-F 9.00-13.00 and 15.30-20.00, Sa 9.00-20.00, Su 9.00-14.00

Another covered (indoor) market that has been resuscitated thanks to the recently opened My Kitch'n (pg. 184), an all organic vegan restaurant and smoothie bar. Founder Jennifer Eric has put together a detoxifying menu of morning smoothies, hearty vegan lunches, and dairy-free desserts. I suggest starting your day with the Green Machine smoothie which will give you the energy you need to explore the city.

A Natural Wine Primer

by Terresa Murphy of La Cucina di Terresa

Terresa is a culinary goddess / vegetarian cooking instructor / natural wine specialist.

I've been teaching vegetarian cuisine in Paris and around the world for many a year, cooking it almost forever. Following the seasons, I'm always thinking of how to prepare vegetables so as not to alter their original nature, simply coaxing out their subtle savor with a bit of garlic, a pinch of lemon zest, a sprinkle of fresh thyme.

In a certain sense you could say I "undress" vegetables, and that's where natural wine—or "naked" wine as some call it—comes in. Vegetable dishes cry out for a naked wine:

mineral echoing mineral, earthy tones and fresh acidity, an undercurrent of *terroir,* all resonating in a subtle balance that simply sings with vegetables.

One day, in 2007, I drove up a tiny road in the Loire Valley, stopped in front of a humble barn of sorts, got out, and entered Joel Courtault's *chai* (wine cellar). That first sip of his natural wine was, well, life altering.

I have since become close to many natural winemakers, who, like Joel, are exuberantly passionate about their *métier*. They are all alchemists of a sort who craft beautiful wines that sing on the palate.

It's a humble recipe: they start with grapes grown organically and biodynamically on small domaines. After hand-picking the grapes at harvest, the winemakers skillfully accompany them as they ferment and "become" wine. No chaptalization (the adding of sugar), no foreign yeasts, no fining or filtration (which means none of the egg, fish, or other animal byproducts that are often used in industrial processes), and little or no sulfites added. For the purists, sulfites are strictly off the table. They leave the grapes to their own natural process, simply escorting them on their voyage. And they then offer to us what I might just call "the drink of the goddesses—and gods."

Among the many wonderful grape varietals nurtured by natural wine-makers in the Loire Valley are Sauvignon, Menu Pineau (Arbois), Chenin, Romorantin, Chardonnay, Melon de Bourgogne, Grolleau, Gamay, Cabernet Franc, Pinot Noir, Pineau d'Aunis, and Cot (Malbec). Coupled with seasonal vegetable dishes, you'll tune into each wine's spicy earthiness, daring mineral tones, tangy acidity, gentle fruit, floating notes of sea and flint.

In Paris, you can sip and shop for natural wines at these *bars à vins* and *cavistes* (which are marked on the arrondissement maps):

Le Garde Robe
Wine bar

☛ 41 Rue de l'Arbre Sec, 1st

Versant Vins
Wine shop

☛ at Marché des Enfants Rouges, 39 Rue de Bretagne, 3rd
↳ Facebook Versant Vins

Septime La Cave
Wine shop and bar

☛ 3 rue Basfroi, 11th (also a restaurant nearby pg.19)

Crus et Découvertes
Wine shop

☛ 7 rue Paul Bert, 11th

Le Siffleur de Ballons
Wine bar & shop

☛ 34 Rue de Cîteaux, 12th
↳ Facebook Le Siffleur de Ballons

Cave des Papilles
Wine shop

☛ 35 rue Daguerre, 14th
↳ www.lacavedespapilles.com/

Le Chapeau Melon
Wine shop (day) & restaurant

☛ 92 Rue Rebeval, 19th

Terresa offers "A Day with a Natural Winemaker" excursions—organic vegetarian cooking class included—in the verdant Loire Valley, where guests get to experience the vineyards, cellars, and kitchens of natural wine-makers. To learn more, see pages 44, 144, 215 and visit
www.lacucinaditerresa.com

Clothes Shopping

Vegan shoes, cosmetics, and more

Paris, so far, has only one 100-percent vegan store (Un Monde Vegan in the 3rd), and it should be on every visitor's travel agenda. But if you have visions of non-leather heels or fashion-forward cruelty-free handbags in your head, you'll want to circle some of the addresses below.

Good Guys Shoes
➤ www.goodguys.fr

Beautifully constructed, fashion-forward vegan shoes designed in Paris, produced in Portugal, and sold in boutiques throughout the French capital. Look for them at stores like Citadium, Wait, Democratie, and Colette.

3rd

Un Monde Vegan
64 rue Notre Dame de Nazareth
see page 67
➤ www. unmondevegan.com

Paris's first vegan storefront is like the Holy Grail of vegan goodness. Any packaged vegan comestible you could ever hope for is here, including cheeses, meats, pâtés, condiments,

and candy bars. It's not all convenience foods, though. There are also vegan leather shoes and belts, but the look is very specific (dark and masculine). A good place to pick up vegan dog treats and even cosmetics.

4th

Lush Cosmetics and Spa
☛ 18 rue Vieille du Temple
www.lush.fr

The Lush cosmetics and bodycare line is mostly vegan and 100-percent vegetarian, and at their Paris spa, you can be on the receiving end of pampering pedicures, relaxing massages, and feel-good facials.

Thrift-store central
☛ rue de la Verrerie between rue des Archives and rue Vieille du Temple

Freepstar, Vintage Bar, and Kilo Shop are just a few of the great spots for scoring sartorial treasures in the Marais. Venture further out and discover even more secondhand boutiques.

10th

Carmen Ragosta
See restaurant listing pg. 132

This friendly boutique in the Canal Saint-Martin neighborhood is Paris's primary distributor of stylish, vegan Melissa shoes.

Plenty of choices for men and women, and worth a stop just to meet Pippo, the adorable shop dog.

Non-leather shoe heaven #1
☞ rue du Faubourg du Temple between blvd Jules Ferry and ave Parmentier

If you don't mind a Made in China label on the bottom of your shoe, you'll probably like browsing among the cheap *ballerines*, boots, and sandals at the many shoe stores on this stretch of the 10th.

13th

Boutique Sagane
☞ 64 ave d'Italie, 13th
🕐 M 14.00-19.30, Tu-Sa 10.30-19.30, Su closed
🔗 www.boutique-sagane.fr
facebook.com/Boutique.Sagane

In January 2014, Paris ushered in a first: An all-vegan purse-and-handbag shop! The ethical vegan owners proudly vend 100-percent synthetic, eco-friendly bags in loads of lovely colors and contemporary styles ranging from casual to super swanky. Besides bags, Boutique Sagane is also a great spot to pick up that Parisian necessity, the parapluie. All of their umbrellas are lightweight and come with a one-year guarantee.

17th

Non-leather shoe heaven #2
☞ Avenue de Clichy between rue Brochant and ave de Saint-Ouen

Loads of cheap shoes-and-clothing stores to be found in this corner of Paris. Look for faux leather shoes, imitation fur and leather jackets, and trendy clothing at the many boutiques lining both sides of the street.

18th

Le Marché Aux Puces Saint-Ouen
☞ Between Porte Saint-Ouen and Porte de Clignancourt
🔗 marcheauxpuces-saintouen.com

This flea market is the closest thing Paris has to London's Camden Market, and getting lost in the back alleys is half the fun. Vintage lovers should make a dash for Chez Sara (Passage Lecuyer), an incredible store full of perfectly preserved vintage dresses, hats, shoes, and more, from the late-1800s to the 1970s. Falbalas (stand 284-285 inside the market's Marché Dauphine) is another treasure trove of vintage garments.

THINGS TO DO

Paris Checklist

There's so much to do and see outside the French capital's major tourist attractions if you take the time to explore.

Make sure to spend time enjoying the city's many beautiful parks (*le pique-nique* is practically a mandatory activity), exploring the covered arcades, and getting acquainted with local people and organizations that share your interest in food, animals, and the environment. And if you need to indulge in a bit of retail therapy, there are plenty of cruelty-free options.

Paris Vegan Day

Paris Vegan Day
▸ www.parisveganday.fr

This semi-annual event brings together thousands of vegans from all over the world in October. Food demos, speakers, dance and music, and lots of food sampling at dozens of booths.

Top Events

Paris hosts a few big veg events each year, and lots of smaller ones in between. These events have a strong Anglophone showing, and are a good place to network and meet new people while you're in France.

VegFest
🏹 www.vegfest.fr

Daylong event near the Georges Pompidou center. A good place to meet local organizations working on behalf of animals. Plus, vegan cupcakes and free food from Loving Hut!

Veggie Pride
🏹 www.veggiepride.org

This annual event was launched in Paris, but now moves to a different European city each year for the middle weekend in May. In 2014, it returned to the City of Light. A great spot to meet animal rights folk.

Salon Bio
🏹 www.vivez-nature.com

Vivez Nature hosts several organic expos in Paris and throughout France. Not entirely veg, but plenty of interest to herbivores here, including booths selling natural products ranging from skin cream to supplements.

Ashtanga Yoga
☛ 40 ave de la République, 11th
   Cross street: av Parmentier
📞 01 45 80 19 96
🏹 www.ashtangayogaparis.fr

One of Paris's longest-established yoga centers offers one week of unlimited English-led yoga classes for €45. All food-related potlucks and other events are vegetarian.

Sivananda Yoga Center
☛ 140 rue du Faubourg Saint-Martin, 10th
🏹 www.sivananda.org/paris

Free yoga class every Saturday from 14.00-15.30. They also offer vegetarian cooking classes on Saturdays. (See pg. 44)

Festivals and Events

There are a million reasons to come to Paris. Here are a few of them:

January/February
Chinese New Year
Retail Sales

March
Le Salon du Livre
Paris Art Fair

April
Paris Marathon
Paris Bridal Fair

May
French Open
Veggie Pride

June
VegFest Paris
Fête de la Musique
Gay Pride
Retail Sales

July
Bastille Day
Paris Plages
Tour de France (below)

August
Rock en Seine
Paris Plages

September
Festival d'Automne
Jazz à la Villette
Les Journées du Patrimoine
Techno Parade

October
Paris Vegan Day
Fête des Vendanges de Montmartre (below)
Nuit Blanche
Vivez Nature
FIAC

November
Salon du Chocolat
Salon Marjolaine
Illuminations De Noël

December
Marchés de Noël

Organizations

Want to get involved in some vegetarian events while you're in Paris? Informal and formal get-togethers are hosted regularly by local organizations ranging from animal rights groups to yoga centers. Brush up on your French and attend an event. Many listed below are actually Anglophone events.

Paris Vegan Meetup
ⓚ meetup.com/Paris-Vegan-Group

Paris's vegan meetup group has more than 1,000 enthusiastic members who host restaurant outings, picnics, book clubs, and other events. Meet local Anglophones like Elisabeth here, and

learn about living vegan in the City of Light. See also the Spicy Vegetarian Social Club with over 700 members

ⓚ meetup.com/vegetarian-475

Association Végétarienne de France
ⓚ www.vegetarisme.fr

France's largest veg organization hosts lectures, film-screenings, and other events with a vegan focus. A great resource for any would-be herbivore in the Francophone world.

L214 Éthique et Animaux
ⓚ www.l214.com

This animal rights organization organizes leafleting events, protests, and other activities that work to end the suffering of food-production animals. Coming to town? See what you can do to help 'em out!

Mangez Végétarien
ⓚ www.mangez-vegetarien.com

This non-profit organization exists to support people on their quest to become vegetarian. They host picnics and meat-out events, and the website is full of information and resources—in French.

AnimaVeg

🏹 www.animaveg.be

This Belgium-based AR/vegan website and forum offers information in French on subjects ranging from animal adoptions to bullfighting protests.

Association Droits des Animaux

🏹 www.droitsdesanimaux.net

A simple website, in French, with news and information about AR legislation in France and throughout Europe.

Fondation Brigitte Bardot

🏹 www.fondationbrigittebardot.fr

The famous French-actress-turned-animal-rights-advocate's organization is great source of inspiration and information. You'll find details on the next anti-fur *manifestations* (demonstrations) listed here, plus animal rights news from around the globe.

One Voice

🏹 www.one-voice.fr

This national animal rights group works hard to defend *les droits des animaux* both in France and throughout Europe using non-violent principles to meet their goals.

Societé Vegane

🏹 www.societevegane.fr

The French arm of the UK Vegan Society works to spread veganism through education, outreach, events, and science-based information.

VegActu

🏹 www.vegactu.com

This vegetarian news site (in French) keeps you up-to-date on all the veg-oriented news happening both in France and around the world.

Vegedia

🏹 www.vegedia.com

A social networking site for vegans and vegetarians. Even if you don't join (it's free), you can access the event calendar and forums, which includes a section on ride-sharing to and from AR/veg events.

Les Vegans de Paris et d'Ailleurs

▸ www.facebook.com/
  groups/124458674285594

Organized by a pair of friendly French women, this organization is working toward the goal of veganizing France through festive events and outings, partnerships with other organizations, and food lobbying.

Cooking Schools

Love food and want to enhance your cooking skills while you're on holiday? Cooking classes have become the *de rigueur* vacation activity for adventurous types in Paris, and the possibilities are vast and varied—think macrobiotic, ayurvedic, and shojin ryori—for vegans and vegetarians alike.

10th

Sivananda Yoga Center

- ☛ 140 rue du Faubourg Saint-Martin
  Cross street: blvd Magenta
- ☎ 01 40 26 77 49
- ⊖ Métro: Gare de l'Est
- ⬩ www.sivananda.org

Learn to prepare Ayurvedic-style meals at these monthly, affordable (€30) bilingual classes. Once a year, the center also offers four day stages (training sessions) in the vegetarian culinary arts.

11th

La Cucina di Terresa

- ☛ Exact locations vary
- ⬩ www.lacucinaditerresa.com
  lacucinaditerresa@gmail.com

Every cooking class and market tour is a full-day experience that takes you from Paris's lively marchés and into a private home where you'll learn to prepare divine veg(an) organic meals with the help of a culinary master. Friendly, warm, and engaging, Terresa inspires with her fabulous recipes and expert skill. Set aside between €125-330 for a memorable, once-in-a-lifetime experience. See also pg.34, 144, 215.

Culinary Messengers

- 3 rue Ternaux
  Cross street: Oberkampf
- 06 10 24 06 53
- Métro: Parmentier

Learn to cook shojin ryori, or Japanese Buddhist temple cuisine, with Valerie Duvauchelle at her monthly ateliers. Valerie, who lived in Japan for 20 years, also works as an independent instructor and caterer, and writes books and articles on vegan zen cuisine. Her blog (lacuisinedevalerie. blogspot.fr).features recipes and food photos. Classes, like the recent Japanese pastry-making workshop, cost €30.

Centre International Macrobiotique Ohsawa (CIMO)

- 8 rue Rochebrune
  Cross street: Parmentier
- 01 48 05 91 35
- Métro: Saint-Amboise
- www.cimo.free.fr

Paris's macrobiotic center hosts twice-monthly vegan cooking classes—in French—where you'll prepare a multi-course meal with a small group of fellow students. Fee: €25.

14th

Chocolatitudes

- 57 rue Daguerre
  Cross street: rue Gassendi
- 01 42 18 49 02
- Métro: Gaîtéor Raspail
- www.chocolatitudes.com

While technically not a *cooking* class, you will develop a taste for chocolate and learn to tell the difference between 70 percent and 82 percent cacao with friendly experts at this vegan-owned chocolate shop in southern Paris. Monthly ateliers last 2 hours, average 6-8 students, and cost €45. Sampling including.

See also pg. 168.

18th

Cook'n with Class

- 6 rue Baudelique
  Cross street: rue Ordener
- 01 42 57 22 84
- Métro: Simplon
- www.cooknwithclass.com

Always wanted to know the secret behind a crunchy, chewy baguette? Take a bread-making—in English—class at this little culinary school on the backside of Montmartre and learn how to make French breads at home. Instruction costs €125 and you get to take home the fruits of your labors.

18th

Super Naturelle

- 34 rue Ramey
  Cross street: rue Custine
- 06 99 63 67 49
- Métro: Jules Joffrin or Chateau Rouge
- www.super-naturelle.com

Learn how to prepare a gourmet vegan brunch or a multi-course Indonesian feast from scratch at this vegan cooking school in the north of Paris. Workshops are held throughout the week and on weekends, and cost between €60 and €80 per session. Half the time is spent in the open, airy kitchen preparing your meal, and the other half is spent savoring the flavors at a sit-down experience shared with your fellow students.

20th

Vegga Bio

- Locations vary
- 06 60 93 20 55
- www.vegga-bio.com
  veggabio@gmail.com

Roving chef and cooking instructor Sébastien Briant teaches vegan, vegetarian, and gluten-free cooking classes throughout Paris. For €50, you'll get three hours of class time and come away with skills that will support you on your quest to create tasty meals at home.

Language Guide

You needn't be fluent in French to enjoy your time in France, but it's really, really helpful to commit a few words to memory to ingratiate yourself to the locals, who'll then help you by speaking in English. (Never mind what you've heard; most people speak English, but they don't always let on that they do.)

Being nice and polite can go a long way. Begin every phrase with "Excusez-moi" or "*Madame/ Monsieur, s'il vous plaît*" and you'll be met with warmth and friendliness that almost always yields positive results.

Navigating Restaurant Menus

These are some of the most common terms you'll encounter at restaurants throughout France.

Je suis	I'm
végétarien(ne)	vegetarian
végétalien(ne)	vegan

Sans produits laitiers	Without dairy
Sans oeufs	Without eggs

La carte – The menu

Formule/Menu – A set meal, which usually includes two options: entrée and main dish, or main dish and dessert. Often a better deal than buying à la carte.

À la carte – Ordering dishes individually rather than as a "formule" or "menu."

Petit déjeuner	Breakfast
Déjeuner	Lunch
Dîner	Dinner
A emporter	Take-away

Le hors-d'oeuvre	Starter
Le plat principal	Main dish
Le dessert	Dessert
Le gâteau	Cake

Les boissons –The drinks

À boire To drink, usually presented as "*quelque chose à boire*?" or "something to drink?"

La carte des vins	Wine list
Une bouteille de vin	A bottle of wine
Un verre	A glass
Rouge	Red
Blanc	White
Brut	Dry
Doux	Sweet

Corsé	Full bodied
Léger	Light
Mousseux	Sparkling, fizzy
Sec	Dry
Une bière	A beer
Le cidre	Cider
Un pichet	small pitcher,
Carafe d'eau	Carafe of tap water

Jus d'orange	Orange juice
La limonade	Lemonade
Avec de la glace / des glaçons	with ice / ice-cubes
Un café	A coffee
Décaféiné	Decaffeinated
Un thé	A tea
L'infusion	Herbal tea
La camomille	Camomile tea
Le thé à la menthe	Mint tea

Safe for Vegans

Abricot	Apricot
Ail *("eye")*	Garlic
Airelle	Cranberry
Algues	Seaweed
Amande	Almond
Amidon	Starch
Ananas	Pineapple
Asperge	Asparagus
Avocat	Avocado
Avoine	Oat
Aubergine	Eggplant
Baguette aux céréal/graine	Baguette with seeds inside
Banane	Banana
Basilic	Basil
Betterave	Beetro
Beurre d'arachides/	Peanut butter
Beurre de cacahuètes	Peanut butter
Beurre végétal	Vegan butter
Blé	Wheat
Brocoli	Broccoli
Cacahuète	Peanut
Cacher	Kosher
Carotte	Carrot
Noix de cajou	Cashew nut
Cassis	Blackcurrant
Céleri	Celery
Cerise	Cherry
Champignon	Mushroom
Chou	Cabbage
Chou-fleur	Cauliflower
Chou(x) de Bruxelles	Brussels sprout(s)
Citron	Lemon
Citrouille	Pumpkin
Concombre	Cucumber
Confiture	Jam
Coriandre	Cilantro/ coriander
Coulis	Fruit reduction sauce
Courgette	Zucchini
Cresson	Watercress
Cru	Raw
Crudités	Raw veg
Cuit	Cooked
Datte	Date
Endive	Chicory
Epinards	Spinach
Épeautre	Spelt
Farci	Stuffed *(as in peppers etc)*
Farine	Flour
Fenouil	Fennel
Figue	Fig
Un fruit	Piece of fruit
Fruits secs	Dried fruit
Galette de sarrasin	Buckwheat crepe *(almost always vegan though might be cooked in butter)*
Germe de soja	Beansprout
Gingembre	Ginger
Graisse végétal	Vegetable oil
Grenade	Pomegranate
Fève	Fava bean
Flageolot	Kidney bean
Fraise	Strawberry
Framboise	Raspberry
Frites	French frieds
Fumé	Smoked
Haricots	Beans
Haricot rouge	Kidney bean
Huile d'olive	Olive oil
Laitue (feuille de)	Lettuce
Laurier	Bay (leaf)
Légumes	Vegetables
Légumineuses	Legumes/ Pulses
Lentilles	Lentils
Levure	Yeast
Maïs	Sweetcorn
Mangue	Mango
Moutarde	Mustard
Mûre	Blackberry
Noix	Nuts
Navet	Turnip
Noisette	Hazelnut
Noix	Walnut
Nouilles	Noodles
Oignon	Onion
Orge	Barley
Origan	Oregano
Pain complet	Wholemeal bread
Pamplemousse	Grapefruit
Panais	Parsnip
Pastèque	Watermelon
Patate douce	Sweet potato
Pâtes	Pasta *(not pâté)*
Pêche	Peach
Persil	Parsley
Petits pois	Peas
Piment	Chilli
Pistache	Pistachio
Poire	Pear
Poireau	Leek
Pois chiche	Chick pea/ Garbanzo
Poivre	Pepper *(condiment)*
Poivron	Peppers (veg)
Pomme	Apple
Pomme de terre	Potato
Potiron	Squash
Pousse	Sprout
Prune	Plum
Pruneau	Prune
Puttanesca	Tomato sauce with peppers and olives
Radis	Radish
Raisin	Grape
Raisin sec	Raisin
Riz	Rice
Riz complet	Brown rice
Romarain	Rosemary
Sauge	Sage
Séché	Dried
Sel	Salt
Semoule	Semolina
Soja	Soy
Sucre	Sugar
Tofu	Tofu
Tomate	Tomato

Tonyu	Soya drink	Truffe	Truffle	Yaourt de soja	Soy yogurt
Tournesol	Sunflower	Vinaigre	vinegar		

Vegetarian, but not vegan

Croissant	Breakfast pastry	Cantal	A common type of cheese	Miel	Honey
Pain au chocolat	Chocolate pastry			Nutella	Hazelnut spread
(both generally made with butter)		Chèvre	Goat cheese		*(made with milk)*
Beurre	Butter	Crème	Cream	Oeuf	Egg
Brebis	Sheep's milk cheese	Ecrèmé	Made with cream	Quiche aux légumes	Vegetable quiche
Café noisette	Coffee with a hint of milk to turn it the color of *noisettes* (hazelnuts)	Fondue	Melted cheese	Tarte Provençale	A pie-like tart *(often cheese- and egg-based, made with Mediterranean vegetables)*
		Fromage	Cheese		
		Gratin	With cheese on top		
		Lait	Milk	Viennoiserie	Breakfast pastries

The Verboten List

A list of things most herbivores will want to avoid. Helpful for restaurant dining, and for reading ingredients lists at grocery stores too.		Croque Madame	Grilled ham, cheese, and egg sandwich	Lardons	Bacon
				Mouton	Mutton
		Dinde	Turkey	Noix de Saint-Jacques	Scallops
		Espadon	Swordfish		
Anchois	Anchovy	Epaule	pork shoulder	Oie	Goose
Agneau	Lamb	Escargot	Snail	Parmentier haché	Hamburger with potatoes
Boeuf	Beef	Faux Filet	Flank steak		
Bolognese	Tomato sauce with meat	Foie	Liver	Poisson	Fish
		Gambas	Shrimp	Porc	Pig
Canard	Duck	Graisse d'oie	Goose fat	Poulpe	Octopus
Croque Monsieur	Grilled ham and cheese sandwich			Poulet	Chicken
		Homard	Lobster	Saumon	Salmon
		Jambon	Ham	Thon	Tuna
		Langoustine	Giant shrimp	Veau	Veal
				Viande	Meat

Extras

Un couteau	A knife	Une Fourchette	A fork	Les toilettes	The bathroom / toilet
Une cuillère	A spoon	Une serviette	Napkin		

Bon appetit!

l'Addition	the bill/check	C'est ma tournée	It's my round
Le montant	total	A votre santé!	Good health!
Le couvert	Cover charge	Santé!	Cheers!
Le pourboire	Tip		
Gardez la monnaie	Keep the change		

1st Arrondissement

The city's first arrondissement stretches east from the Tuileries gardens toward the Marais, stopping just short of Paris's best modern art museum, the Centre Georges Pompidou.

Inside this giant rectangular district, you'll discover the always-overwhelming (in a good way) Louvre, the Palais-Royal and its pretty manicured gardens, and a dozen covered passages offering myriad eating-and-shopping possibilities.

This is prime Paris window-shopping territory, so wear your walking shoes and be prepared to work up an appetite.

Vegetarian/Neighborhood pick

Saveurs Veget'halles
Vegetarian restaurant

- 📍 41 rue Bourdonnais
  Cross street: rue de Rivoli
- ☎ 01 40 41 93 95
- ⊖ Métro: Chatelet-Les Halles
- 🕐 M–Sa 12.00–15.00 and 18.30–23.00, Su closed
- 🔗 www.saveursvegethalles.fr

This welcoming restaurant is 90-percent vegan, and a relaxed spot for dinner with friends or a leisurely weekday lunch. The food is "French," meaning that pâtés, terrines, and big salads feature prominently.

Try the Escalope de Seitan or the Assiette Composé—the culinary equivalent of a trip to a health spa—and don't miss the terrine de champignon served with onion chutney.

Wine is served, as well as desserts like vegan crème brulée, carrot cake, and fruit crumbles.

Lots of gluten-free options to choose from, too, including beer.

Prices for the mid-day *formule* (first course, main course, dessert) run €15.90; the evening *formule* is €18.90.

Terrace seating. Credit cards accepted.

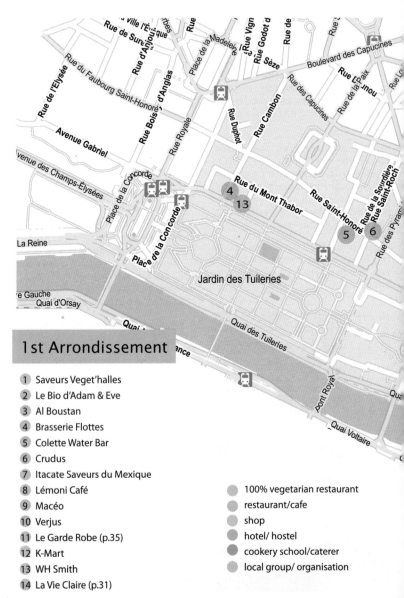

1st Arrondissement

1 Saveurs Veget'halles
2 Le Bio d'Adam & Eve
3 Al Boustan
4 Brasserie Flottes
5 Colette Water Bar
6 Crudus
7 Itacate Saveurs du Mexique
8 Lémoni Café
9 Macéo
10 Verjus
11 Le Garde Robe (p.35)
12 K-Mart
13 WH Smith
14 La Vie Claire (p.31)

100% vegetarian restaurant
restaurant/cafe
shop
hotel/ hostel
cookery school/caterer
local group/ organisation

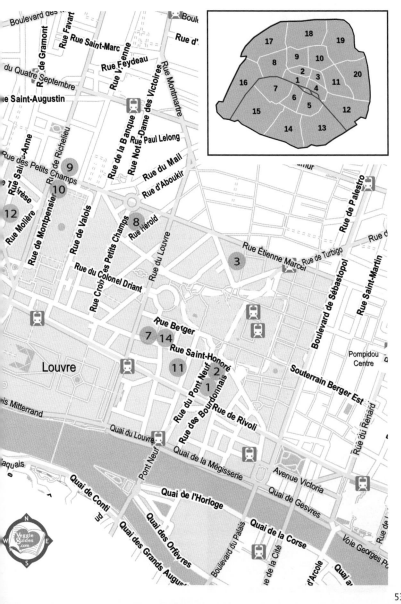

Le Bio d'Adam & Eve
Omnivorous healthy

- 41 rue Saint-Honoré
  Cross street: rue des Bourdonnais
- 09 82 36 94 57
- Métro: Chatelet or Les Halles
- M-Sa 11.30-20.00, Su closed; closed throughout August
- www.lebiodadameteve.com
  Facebook Le Bio d'Adam et Eve

This little three-in-one café-smoothie bar-mini health-food market makes a great pit-stop after an afternoon shopping at Les Halles.

Dairy-free smoothies, organic juices, and sandwiches are made on-the-spot, and a deli case offers many premade options for takeaway. Grab one of the few tables, take a plate, see what's available at the hot buffet, which might include including seitan parmentier, soba noodles with veggies, or a tomatoey lasagna (sold by weight). Side salads (€2.99), coffee (€1), and a variety of desserts including dairy-free milkshakes and muffins.

Gluten-free goods are available throughout the day. Credit cards accepted.

Al Boustan
Omnivorous Lebanese

- 21 rue Montorgueil
  Cross street: rue Étienne-Marcel
- 01 40 41 02 40
- Métro: Étienne-Marcel
- M-Su 11.00-00.00
  www.alboustan.fr

Situated on a lively pedestrian street a few paces from the Les Halles shopping district, Al Boustan offers a taste of the Middle East at great prices. Tuck into a tasty vegetarian *formule* composed of 10 different plant-based delicacies (€15), or choose an à la carte buffet of warm and hot dishes including eggplant salad (€2.20), falafel (€1.30), hummus (€2.20), and fava beans with lemon and olive oil (€2.20).

Wine and Lebanese pastis served, as well as a variety of non-alcoholic beverages. Terrace seating. Credit cards accepted.

Brasserie Flottes
Omnivorous French

- 2 rue Cambon
  Cross street : rue de Rivoli
- 01 42 60 80 89
  Métro: Concorde
- M-Su 7.00-00:30
- www.brasserie-flottes.com

Across the street from the Tuileries gardens, just off the celebrated rue de Rivoli (the last stop of the annual Tour de France race), Brasserie Flottes is a very traditional French café that manages to be accessible to vegetarians — as long as they don't mind dining next to the guy eating steak tartare.

All meat-free items are marked with a green circle, including vegetable soup (€9.80), green detox salad (€16.50), and fusilli with cherry tomatoes (€15.50). If you like fancy fried foods, you might want to spring for the truffled *frites* (€12), and for dessert, there's a nice selection of Berthillon vegan sorbets.

Terrace seating. Free wifi. Credit cards accepted.

Colette Water Bar
Omnivorous healthy

- ☛ 213 rue Saint-Honoré
  Cross street: rue de Richelieu
  01 55 35 33 90
- ⊖ Métro: Palais Royal-Musée du Louvre, Pyramides & Tuileries
- 🕐 M-Su 12-19.00
- ⚲ www.colette.fr

This hyper trendy clothing store draws the chicest Parisians and world-travelers, and the downstairs Water Bar is where they — and you — fill up between purchases.

Try the tabouli, falafel, and hummus plate (€15.50), the fresh gazpacho (€9), or the vitality salad, and finish with a vegan sorbet (€8) for dessert.

As its name implies, the stylish cantine also sells a variety of waters and other drinks, plus snacks to-go. Credit cards accepted.

Crudus
Omnivorous Italian

- ☛ 21 rue Saint-Roch
  Cross street: rue du Faubourg Saint-Honoré
- 📞 01 42 60 90 29
- ⊖ Métro: Pyramides, Tuileries
- 🕐 M-F 12.00-14.30 and 19.00-23.00, Sa-Su closed
- ⚲ www.crudus.wix.com/crudus

Organic Italian you say? Si, per favore! This is elegant dining in Paris's fashionable heart. Cosy and intimate, it's a nice spot to share mushroom fricassée (€17), pasta stuffed with pumpkin (€17), or linguini with truffles (€40) with someone you love (or at least like a lot). Top-notch service and a great location within walking distance of the Louvre and Opéra Garnier make this worth the trek. Credit cards accepted

Itacate Saveurs du Mexique
Omnivorous Mexican

- ☛ 94 rue Saint Honoré
  Cross street: rue de l'Arbre Sec
- 📞 01 42 33 39 87
- ⊖ Métro: Louvre-Rivoli
- 🕐 M-F 12.00-15.00 and 18.30-22.00, Sa 12.00-23.00, Su closed
- ⚲ www.itacate.fr
  Facebook Itacate Saveurs du Mexique

One of Paris's newest Mexican restaurants is also one of its most veg-friendly. A self-described taqueria (taco shop), here you'll find all the things you come to expect at a Mexican eatery: The rice-based drink horchata (€2.50), guacamole and chips (€6.50), and tacos (3 for €8), among others. Lunch *formule* is €12.50, and includes rice or beans, tacos and quesadilla, and a drink.

Margaritas (€5.50) and Mexican beers (€5–6). Outdoor seating and a lively vibe. Credit cards accepted.

Lémoni Café
Omnivorous Greek

- ☛ 5 rue Herold
  Cross street: rue Étienne Marcel
- ☏ 01 45 08 49 84
- ⊖ Métro: Palais Royale
- ◕ M–F 12.00–15.30
- ↖ www.lemonicafe.fr

The theme of this cute café's cuisine is "healthy Cretan" — meaning no butter, refined sugars, crème or cow's milk products. Instead, look for Greek-inspired salads including tabouli, lentil, and the summery cucumber-watermelon.

One or two veg hot items are offered daily, including soup. The sandwich *formule* (€10) might include a veggie-stuffed wrap, salad, and a drink; the plat *formule* (€18.50) includes a choice of warm dishes and a house-made dessert. Veggie burgers, and savory "cakes" are other possibilities.

Beer and wine served. Credit cards accepted.

Macéo
Omnivorous French fusion

- ☛ 15 rue des Petites Champs
  Cross street: rue de Richelieu
- ☏ 01 42 97 53 85
- ⊖ Métro: Pyramides
- ◕ M–F 9.00–00, Sa 17.00–00.00, Su closed; closed throughout August
- ↖ www.maceorestaurant.com

You can't miss Maceo — its flashy, bright-red exterior acts like a beacon. Inside you can expect attentive staff, comfortable décor, and a Parisian ambience.

The vegetarian menu is extensive, and many items can be veganized. Look for dishes like grilled spring vegetables with tomato confit (€19) and basil risotto with pine nuts (€22).

Oenophiles will appreciate the extensive wine list, and teetotalers have juice, coffee, and other drinks to choose from. Credit cards accepted.

Verjus
Omnivorous French fusion

- 52 Rue de Richelieu
  Cross street: rue des Petits Champs
- 01 42 97 54 40
- Métro: Pyramides
- M-F 18.00–23.00; closed weekends
- www.verjusparis.com

Upscale dining that's vegan-friendly, a short walk from the Louvre, Palais-Royal, and Opera Garnier.

Try the multi-course, off-the-menu vegan tasting menu (€60) based on seasonal vegetables is also available with a wine-pairing option (€100), which is recommended.

Call ahead for special dietary requests; English spoken. Can be off-the-charts noisy, but the downstairs wine bar is a much quieter (and less expensive) option. Credit cards accepted.

K-Mart
Omnivorious Asian supermarket

- 6-8 rue Sainte Anne
  Cross street: ave de l'Opéra
- 01 58 63 49 09
- Métro: Pyramides
- M-Sa 10–21.00, Su closed

Americans might be confused by this Japanese-Korean grocery store's name; you will not find discounted clothing or household goods here like you would at the big box stateside chain, but you will discover all kinds of tasty edible treats to take away, including fresh veg sushi, pickled vegetables, rice and noodle dishes, and more.

In the packaged foods section, you can fill your basket with natto (fermented soybeans eaten as a snack) and sweet mochi cakes for dessert. This is also a good spot to load up on noodle bowls, if you plan to eat some of your meals or snacks in your hotel room. Credit cards accepted

WH Smith
Omnivorous bookstore

☛ 248 rue de Rivoli
Cross street: Cambon

☏ 01 44 77 88 99

⊖ Métro: Concorde

🕐 M-Sa 9.00-19.00, Su 12.30-19.00

↖ www.whsmith.fr

Paris's biggest English-language bookstore seems an unlikely spot for sourcing vegetarian food, but upstairs in the mini *épicerie*, you'll find all kinds of goodies to snack on.

Try the Marmite-flavored rice cakes (€1.40) and Marmite cashews (€4.40), or skip the vehicle and go straight for the source with a jar of the sticky stuff. (Australians will be happy to know they sell Vegemite too.)

Look for tea, jam, Dorset breakfast cereals, and four different varieties of Nature's Path gluten-free cereals.

For dessert, there are Divine dark chocolate bars (€2-3.60) and plenty of other English- and American-style junk foods.

Credit cards accepted.

2nd Arrondissement

Paris's second arrondissement sits square in the middle of the city's key financial district, and the dining possibilities lean toward lunch-time, fast-casual spots that cater to the suited-up workforce.

Tourists come to explore the scads of covered arcades that dot the neighborhood, and to catch performances at the many theaters and concert halls.

Spend an afternoon roaming the city's interesting Japantown, and when you've worked up an appetite, you can choose between Asian cuisine, English tea, burgers and fries, or light and healthy salads.

Vegetarian Neighborhood favorite

Vegitai
Vegetarian fusion

- 🖝 39–42 Passage Choiseul
  Cross Street: rue des Petits Champs
- ☏ 09 83 03 62 30
- ⊖ Métro: Quatre Septembre or Pyramides
- 🕔 M–Sa 8.00–18.00
- ⌕ www.facebook.com/Vegitai

Daily specials at this new-ish veg lunch spot with a fast-food vibe are priced right (€7.40) and include rice bowls with fake chicken and vegetables, rice noodles with faux ham, and even fake duck with perfumed rice.

Other options include the daily wraps (€5.50), including one with avocado and "chicken."

Smoothies and green drinks, and a variety of desserts. More vegan desserts to be added in 2014. Credit cards accepted.

PLAT MAISON

NOUILLES DE PATATES DOUCES
SAUTÉES AU CANARD
ET LÉGUMES VARIÉS

7.40€

2nd Arrondissement

1. Vegitai
2. A Priori Thé
3. BioBoa
4. Bio Burger
5. Elgi Bourse (10 rue Saint-Marc)
6. Elgi Montorgeuil (64 rue Montmartre)
7. Fée Nature
8. Juji-Ya
9. Little Seoul
10. Le Pain Quotidien
11. Qualité & Co.
12. Brentano's American bookshop

- 100% vegetarian restaurant
- restaurant/cafe
- shop
- hotel/ hostel
- cookery school/caterer
- local group/ organisation

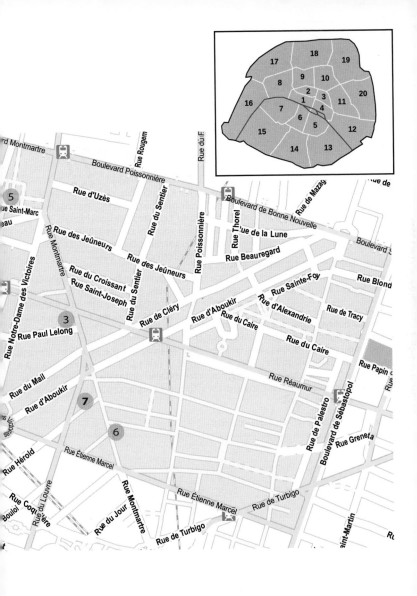

A Priori Thé
Omnivorous English fusion

- 35–37 Galerie Vivienne/6 rue des Petits Champs
  Cross street: rue Vivienne
- 01 42 97 48 75
- Métro: Bourse
- M–F 12.00–18.00; Sa–Su 12.00–18.00
- www.apriorithe.com

An American owner and an English-style tea-room specials are what's on the menu at this beautiful spot in the picturesque Belle Epoque covered passageway.

Come for tea and coffee, salads, sweet and savory tarts, and a nice selection of homemade baked goods.

After you've enjoyed a leisurely Sunday brunch that includes a hot beverage, fresh juice, scones and jam, main course, and dessert (€30), wander the famous gallery and poke your nose into the shops ranging from lose-yourself-for-an-hour toy stores to upscale wine shops.

Terrace seating. Credit cards accepted.

BioBoa
Omnivorous healthy

- 93 rue Montmartre
  Cross street: rue Réamur
- 01 40 28 02 83
- Métro: Sentier or Bourse
- M 11.00–16.00, T–F 11.00–16.00 and 19.00–00.00, Su 11.00–16.00
- www.bioboa.fr

Stir- fried tofu and veggies (€17), veggie burger (€15), gazpacho (€7), and Lebanese tabouli salad (€8) are just some of the possibilities awaiting discerning herbivores at this hip, modern organic café.

Wines available by the glass (€4.50–9) and bottle (€23–90), and a number of fresh-pressed juice options, including carrot–orange–lime (€7) to quench your thirst.

Prefer to eat in the shade of a plane tree in one of Paris's parks? Pick up a fresh salad or sandwich for takeaway. Credit cards accepted.

Bio Burger
Omnivorous burgers

- 46 Passage Choiseul
  Cross Street: rue des Petits Champs
- 01 49 26 93 90
  Métro: Quatre Septembre or
- Pyramides
- M–F 11.30–15.30, Sa 11.30–16.00; closed Sundays
- www.bioburger.fr

Everything on the menu at this fast-food eatery in the airy Passage Choiseul is organic (*bio*), from the burger and bun right down to the ketchup and mustard.

Every burger (€7–8) on the menu can be made vegan—including the barbecue burger with onion confit and grilled eggplant. The meatless burger base is soy grown in southwest France.

Fries, salad, and a variety of hot and cold drinks on offer (€1.20–2.50), plus a daily "formule" that includes a burger, salad or fries, and drink or dessert for €10.50.

The spot is small, but there's upstairs seating and a couple of spots on the "terrace." Kid-friendly. Credit cards accepted. A second location with a similar menu just opened at 10 rue de la Victoire in the 9th.

Elgi (two locations)
Omnivorous healthy

- 10 rue Saint-Marc
  Cross street: rue Vivienne
- Métro: Bourse
- M–F 11:30–15.30
- www.elgi.fr

- 64 rue Montmartre
  Cross street: rue du Louvre
- Métro: Sentier
- M–F 11:30–15.30, Sa 11.30–16.00
- www.elgi.fr

This chain lunch spot can be a lifesaver for hungry vegetarians roaming the streets of the French capital.

Choose a salad base—rice, pasta, or greens—and add dressing and toppings like olives, cucumber, grilled vegetables, beans or nuts to make your custom-order meal (€9–11).

A variety of breads, soups (€4–6) and sandwiches (€8), and smoothies to choose from.

Credit cards accepted.

Fée Nature
Omnivorous healthy

- 🐁 69 rue d'Argout
  Cross street: rue du Louvre
- ☎ 01 42 21 44 36
- ⊖ Métro: Sentier
- ◕ M-F 12.00-18.00; closed weekends
- ↖ www.feenature.com

Mostly vegetarian, and vegan-friendly, this sweet spot is perfect for a lunch on the go.

Several *formules* to choose from: The Salad+Dessert+Drink combo (€9.50) is a light choice, while heartier appetites might opt for the Assiette (€12.50) and tuck into a bit of everything, which might include a vegan tart with eggplant and tomato; arugula salad with red and white quinoa; and soba noodles with roast squash.

Vegan and gluten-free dessert options (€2-4.50), organic tea (€3.80), and organic fruits and vegetable juices (€5), too.

Terrace seating. Credit cards accepted.

Juji-Ya
Omnivorous Japanese

- 🐁 46 rue Sainte Anne
  Cross-street: rue des Petits Champs
- ☎ 01 42 86 02 22
- ⊖ Métro: Quatre Septembre or Pyramides
- ◕ M-S 10.00-22.00, Su 10.00-21.00
- ↖ www.otodoke.fr

Part cantine, part grocery-store, this little gem offers a delicious veg bento box lunch (€10.30) with a brown rice option.

Among the tasty, authentic veg options are kobucha squash, stuffed tofu skin, seaweed salad, sautéed eggplant, and cold noodle salad.

Green tea and Japanese beer also served.

Kid-friendly. Credit cards accepted.

Little Seoul
Omnivorous Korean

- ☛ 19 Passage Choiseul
  Cross street: rue des Petits
  Champs
- ☎ 01 47 03 06 14
- ⊖ Métro: Quatre Septembre or
  Pyramides
- ◑ M–Sa 11.30–19.00; closed
  Sundays

This friendly little spot with upstairs seating offers a fair selection of possibilities for vegans and vegetarians alike, including miso ramen (€7.50), the famous Korean veg-and-rice dish called Bibimbap (€9.90), and a noodle and veggie bowl called japche jeombap (€11.50).

The complete menu includes kimchi and your choice of soup, salad, or dumplings. Japanese and Korean beers, wine, tea, and other drinks available.

Kid-friendly. Credit cards accepted.

Le Pain Quotidien
Omnivorous Mediterranean

- ☛ 5 rue des Petits Champs
  Cross street: rue Vivienne
- ☎ 01 42 60 15 24
- ⊖ Métro: Pyramides or Bourse
- ◑ M–Su 8.00–22.00
- ↖ www.lepainquotidien.com

Vegan and vegetarian items are plentiful and clearly marked at this "healthy" Belgian chain restaurant with an open and airy vibe.

Most dishes come with the trademark "pain" (bread) served with a variety of jams and spreads, including the hummus-heavy Mediterranean mezze plate (€14) . Tartines (open-faced sandwiches), soups, and salads are filling, if a little on the expensive side.

Organic wine served, as well as juice, coffee, and tea.

Kid friendly. Credit cards accepted.

Qualité & Co. (2nd)
Omnivorous healthy

- ☛ 4 rue Choiseul
  Cross street: rue Quatre
  Septembre
- ☎ 01 40 15 09 99
- ⊖ Métro: Quatre September
- ◑ M–Sa 8.30–17.00
- ↖ www.qualiteandco.com

Specializing in nutritious, balanced meals for health-conscious diners, this fast-casual spot offers a nice selection of vegan salads, plus mushroom risotto, and veg lasagna.

The Tarte Provençal (€8.60) comes with a side salad, and the organic quinoa salad offers a fresh mix of peas, beans, apple and nuts (€3.90). For something heartier, go for the grilled vegetable panini (€6.80).

Delectable New Tree chocolate bars are available too.

Free wifi. Credit cards accepted. Also in the 8th, pg 116.

Zen Zoo
Omnivorous Asian

☛ 13 rue Chabanais/2 rue
   Cherubini
   Cross street: Sainte-Anne
☎ 01 42 96 27 28
⊖ Métro: Quatre-Septembre or
   Pyramides
● M–Sa 12.00–19.00; Su closed
↖ www.zen-zoo.com

If the thought of washing down your
tofu-skin rolls (€14, as part of a lunch
special) with a slurpy glass of bubble
tea sounds appealing, you'll love Zen
Zoo, a Taiwanese-style café serving
a variety of veg-friendly snacks.

Upstairs seating and a casual vibe in
which to enjoy your afternoon snack
service (€8.50–13) that includes a
drink and either pastry or dim sum
and bubble tea (or all three).

Credit cards accepted

3rd Arrondissement

The third arrondissement offers an eclectic range of things to do and see.

From rue Rambuteau in the thick of the Marais, stretching north up to the newly revamped Place de la République, you'll discover one of the city's Chinatown districts, oodles of galleries hosting bi-monthly vernissages (art openings), trendy boutiques, a few museums (Picasso, Arts et Métiers, Centre Georges Pompidou), and plenty of opportunities to eat, drink, and be merry.

Pick a sunny day and wander the old streets, getting lost in secret gardens, exploring the crooked side-streets, and partaking in that old Parisian custom, people-watching.

Vegan/Neighborhood favorite

Un Monde Vegan
Vegan shop

- ☞ 64 rue Notre-Dame de Nazareth
  Cross street: Rue de Saint-Martin
- ☏ 01 42 77 49 58
- ⊖ Métro: Republique or Temple
- 🕐 M-W 12.00-19.00, Th-Sa 12.00-20.00
- ⚑ www.unmondevegan.com
  Faceook Un Monde Vegan

This fabulous little vegan oasis began as a mail-order operation and went big in 2012 with its storefront on a quiet street in the northern Marais district.

The best spot in Paris to stock up on faux meat and vegan cheese. VBites products from the UK include Thai-style crab cakes and chicken nuggets, and every scrumptious variety of Vegusto cheeses from Switzerland.

Un Monde Vegan also vends goodies for people with a serious sweet tooth, including Bonvita Bonbarrs and GoMaxGo bars in tempting peanut-butter cup and Snickers-style flavors.

Credit cards accepted.

3rd Arrondissement

- 100% vegetarian restaurant
- restaurant/cafe
- shop
- hotel/ hostel
- cookery school/caterer
- local group/ organisation

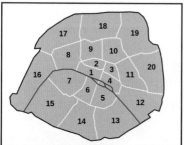

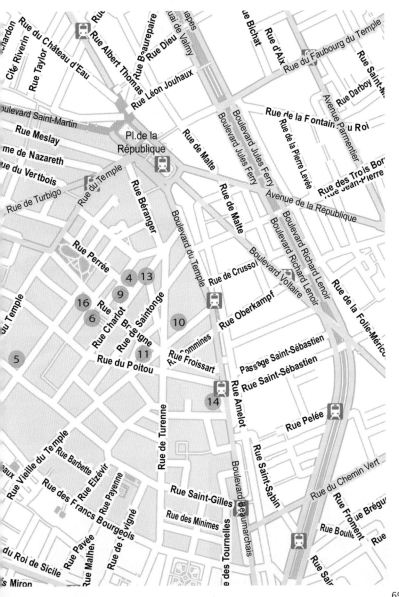

Le Potager du Marais
Vegan restaurants

- 24 rue Rambuteau
  Cross street: rue de Beaubourg
- (01 57 40 98 57
- ⊖ Métro: Rambuteau
- W–Su 12.00–16.00 and 19.00–00.00
- www.lepotagerdumarais.fr

One of Paris's oldest and quaintest vegetarian eateries recently revamped its menu so it's now vegan and mostly gluten-free.

The hazelnut roast with mushrooms and green pepper reduction (€19) comes with either rice, quinoa, or mashed potatoes seasoned with garlic and olive oil. Mushroom pâté (€8) tastes divine spread on crusty bread, and the hearty seitan bourguignon (€18) comes with a rich red-wine sauce.

For dessert, dig into the dairy-free crème brulée with ginger (€8.50) or the creamy chocolate mousse (€7).

Champagne, cider, and natural sodas available, as well as an authentic, old-fashioned hot chocolate (€6).

Credit cards accepted. Terrace seating.

Photos Rebecca Gilbert/ Yummy Plants

Bob's Kitchen
Vegetarian restaurant

- ☛ 74 rue des Gravilliers
  Cross street: blvd du Beaubourg
- ☏ 09 52 55 11 66
- ⊖ Métro: Rambuteau or Arts et Métiers
- ◕ M–F 8.00–15.00, Sa–Su 10.30–16.00. May be closed in August.
- ⚲ www.bobsjuicebar.com

Expect communal tables, daily juice specials (€4–€7.50), lots of attractive model-types, and a vaguely New York vibe—which might be on account of all the English being spoken here.

Lunch menu varies (check the wall for the daily specials) from day to day, but might include a brown-rice bowl with veggies or a veggie stew du jour (€8.50), or a fully-loaded bagel sandwich.

Gluten-free pancakes, nori rolls, and dessert-options aplenty.

Several choices for vegans. It can get really crowded during peak dining hours, so be prepared to wait or opt for takeaway instead.

Credit cards accepted. Kid-friendly. Other branches in the 10th and 18th.

Café Pinson (3rd)
Vegetarian restaurant

- ☛ 6 rue du Forez
  Cross street: rue Charlot
- ☏ 09 83 82 53 53
- ⊖ Métro: Filles du Calvaire
- ◕ M–F 09.00–24.00, Sa 10.00–24.00, Su 12.00 –18.00
- ⚲ www.cafepinson.fr

A lot of money went into creating a chic, homey ambience at this Northern Marais hot spot, but the food's pretty good too. With the exception of one or two items that contain eggs, the menu is vegan.

Sunday brunch is an event (€25), but regulars come for a relaxing weekday fixed-price lunch or dinner that might include a raw gazpacho; sautéed rice with mushrooms, pistachios, and miso-ginger sauce; and apricot tart with cardamom cream.

The owner has food sensitivities and launched this restaurant to serve others like her. A great spot for people with gluten allergies.

A la carte meals begin at €12.50. Credit cards accepted. Kid-friendly. Also in the 10th.

HANK (Have A Nice Karma)
American-style vegan fast food

- 📢 55 rue des Archives
  Cross street: rue des Quatre Fils
- ☎ 09 72 44 03 99
- ⊖ Métro: Rambuteau
- 🕐 Su, Tu 12.00–15.00; W–F
  12.00–15.00, 19.00–21.00;
  Sa 12.00–21.00; M closed
- ⬩ www.hankrestaurant.com

A spate of New York-style burger bars has opened in Paris, and the newest to hit the scene is HANK. Launched by three passionate herbivores who want to make the world a better place one meat-free burger at a time,.

HANK offers good value for your euro. The daily special includes a burger, drink, and dessert, and clocks in at €11, though à la carte options are also available.

Fries are organic, and the burgers come with inventive names and gourmet touches, like l'Aristocrate, served with a truffle sauce.

Credit cards accepted. Tip: Skip the museum across the street, which is filled with dead animals and antique hunting weapons.

Chez Omar
Omnivorous North African

- 📢 47 rue de Bretagne
  Cross street: rue des Archives or rue Charlot
- ☎ 01 42 72 36 26
- ⊖ Métro: Arts et Métiers or Filles du Calvaire
- 🕐 M–Sa 12.00–14.30 and 19.00–23.30; Su 19.00–23.30

With its wood-paneled walls and white tablecloths, this Northern Marais institution looks like the classic French bistro at first glance, but is actually the city's most celebrated couscous restaurant. The vegetable couscous (€12), which is served with a fresh, tasty, vegetable-laden tureen of spiced vegetables, is delish and filling. Mint tea (€2) and North African wines are the stars of the drinks menu. A favorite spot among musicians, actors, and other celebrity types, expect to see and be seen at Omar's. Cash only.

Happy Nouilles
Omnivorous Chinese

- 📍 95 rue Beaubourg
  Cross Street: rue de Turbigo
- 📞 01 44 59 31 22
- ⊖ Métro: Arts et Métiers
- 🕐 M–Sa 12.00–15.00 and 18.30–22:30
- 🔗 www.happynouilles.com/

An omnivorous restaurant with a decent selection of vegan offerings.

The specialty here is the homemade noodles, which they'll whip up into a vegan stir-fry, or a slurptastic noodle soup (€6.90) that goes great with Chinese greens with garlic (€6.00) and a bottle of Tsingtao beer (€3.50). Other vegan dishes include tofu with vegetables and sautéed bok choy and black mushrooms.

Wine, soda, and soy milk available, and the staff are very friendly and eager to please vegetarian customers. Credit cards accepted.

Café Loustic
Omnivorous café

- 📍 40 rue Chapon
  Cross street: rue de Beaubourg
- 📞 09 80 31 07 06
- ⊖ Métro: Arts et Metiers
- 🕐 M 12.00– 18.00, T–F 8.00–18.00, S 9.00–19.00, Su 11.00–18.00
- 🔗 www.facebook.com/cafeloustic

This trendy little café with an English-speaking, on-site proprietor has a hipster vibe and attitude to match, but it's a good place to go for a strong cup of drip coffee (€3) and a slice of the daily vegan cake.

Some days, kale salad is featured on the short menu; call in advance to confirm, and ask for the no-cheese option if you're vegan.

Brunch (€10–12) includes granola (soy milk available on request), juice, coffee, and an array of sweet and savory tarts. Credit cards accepted.

Nanashi
Omnivorous Japanese

☛ 57 rue Charlot
Cross street: rue du Forez
☎ 09 60 00 25 59
⊖ Métro: Filles du Calvaire
🕐 M–Sa 12.00–00.00, Su 12.00–18.00

Bento fever has officially gripped Paris, and Nanashi was one of the forerunners of the craze. Across the street from Café Pinson, this very popular Japanese cantine and bento bar offers three different price structures: To-go (€10), dine-in (€14), and evening/weekends (€16).

Vegetarians can choose from tasty daily offerings including tofu galette with eggplant or a salad of potatoes, fennel, red onion and zucchini.

Two more locations in Paris (6th and 10th) to choose from, too.

Neo Bento
Omnivorous Japanese

☛ 5 rue des Filles du Calvaire
Cross street: blvd du Temple or rue de Bretagne
☎ 09 83 87 81 86
⊖ Métro: Filles du Calvaire
🕐 M–W–Th 11:30–19:30, F–S 11:30–21.30, Su 11.30–16.30
↖ www.neobento.com

Here you get to fill your bento box (€12) with six tasty choices from the extensive veg menu.

Among the possibilities are sweet potato–coconut milk curry; quinoa risotto with truffle oil; soba noodles; marinated zucchini; wasabi broccoli; sprout salad; and coconut tapioca pudding.

This is light food that makes you feel energized and ready to tackle museums and sightseeing. Kid-friendly (game table).

Rose Bakery II
Omnivorous English fusion

☛ 30 rue Debelleyme
Cross dtreet: rue de Bretagne
☎ 01 49 96 54 01
⊖ Métro: Filles du Calvaire
🕐 Tu–Su 9.00–19.00; closed Mondays

British-influenced sweets like fruitcake and scones beckon from behind a glass case, while savory comestibles—including tarts, quiches, and vegetable plates—offer equal allure for salt-loving palates. Come for breakfast, lunch, or takeaway. Serves a good selection of tea and coffee to keep you buzzed and happy all day.

Rose Bakery is well-known for their Sunday brunch and generous portions; the Assiette Legumes (€16) is big enough for two and one of the few vegan options. Other veg possibilities include the tarte du jour and salad plate; pizette and salad; a daily soup; and risotto.

Gluten-free options available. Kid

friendly. Credit cards accepted.

See also pg. 22. Other branches in the 9th (pg.126) and 12th (pg.157).

Vert Midi
Omnivorous healthy

- 🐖 9 rue aux Ours
  Cross street: blvd du Sebastopol
- ☎ 01 42 71 64 36
- ⊖ Métro: Rambuteau or Etienne-Marcel
- 🕐 M-Sa 7.30-16.00; closed weekends
- ↘ www.vertmidi.net

This two-location chain (the second is at 1 rue Saint Marc, 2nd) offers a delicious salad bar where you choose your base—greens, quinoa, pasta—then let the salad maestro add toppings, which vary in price from €1 for mushrooms or beets to €2 for grilled vegetables or sun-dried tomatoes.

Other veg options include soupe du jour (€3) which might be a green gazpacho or tangy tomato-basil, empanadas (€2.90) stuffed with in-season veggies, and fresh-pressed juice from the juice bar (prices begin at €2.70).

Formules range from €8 for the Salade spéciale (salade du jour and juice du jour) to €11.50 for the Plat formule, which includes the soup du jour, hot daily special, and a drink.

Breakfast items include tartines, viennoiserie, and that French morning specialty, hot chocolate.

Credit cards accepted.

La Cantine Merci
Omnivorous French restaurant

- 🐖 111 boulevard Beaumarchais
  Cross street: Saint-Sébastien
- ☎ 01 42 77 79 28
- ⊖ Métro: Saint-Sébastien-Froissart
- 🕐 M-Sa 12.00-18.00, Su closed
- ↘ www.merci-merci.com/en

The restaurant at Paris's premier concept store is a good bet for herbivores who are too tired to cross the street over to Loving Hut (or who want a glass of wine with their meal, which you can't get at Loving Hut).

Gorgeous composed salads brimming with fresh grains and vegetables; flavorful soups; risottos, and luscious berry crumbles for dessert.

Juices run €6.50, main plates between €10-19, and daily menus ring in at €22. Credit cards accepted.

4th Arrondissement

This corner of the Marais is both the gay epicenter and the ancient Jewish quarter, which makes for an interesting mix. Throw in a heaping helping of tourists, vintage clothing stores, secret gardens, and a few museums, and you've got a recipe for a fabulous day-into-night outing.

Don't miss the Musée Carnavelet, with its manicured garden and interesting mélange of art. Maison Victor Hugo is another mustn't-miss; dedicated to the renowned author, this free museum features letters, paintings, furniture, and other memorabilia.

Sundays are perfect for a stroll through the St. Paul shopping district, with its hodge-podge of galleries, book stores, and junk shops.

And finally, a pique-nique at Paris's oldest square, Place des Vosges, is another 4th arrondissement rite of passage. If you're lucky, street musicians will be playing old Django Reinhart tunes under the eaves while you dine en plein air.

Vegan/Neighborhood favorite

Café Ginger
Vegan restaurant

- 9 rue Jacques Coeur
  Cross street: blvd Henri IV
- 01 42 72 43 83
- Métro: Bastille
- Tu-Su 12:30-16:00, also F-Su 19.00-22.00, M closed; check Facebook for occasional closures such as in August
- www.cafe-ginger.fr
  Facebook Café Ginger Paris

The owners of this charming restaurant are trying to go vegan, so they revamped their previously vegetarian menu into a totally egg- and dairy-free affair. Meals are still filling, balanced, and scrumptious.

Dish of the day €12.50. Formules (€16/19.50/23) allow you to choose from a selection of daily tarts, salads, soups, and desserts. Chocolate lovers musn't miss the decadent chocolate "slab" if it's on offer.

Organic wine, tea, coffee, fresh juices, and hot chocolate are available, as are gluten-free options.

One of the owners is English, and if he's on hand, he can explain menu options.

Terrace seating. Dog-friendly. Credit cards accepted.

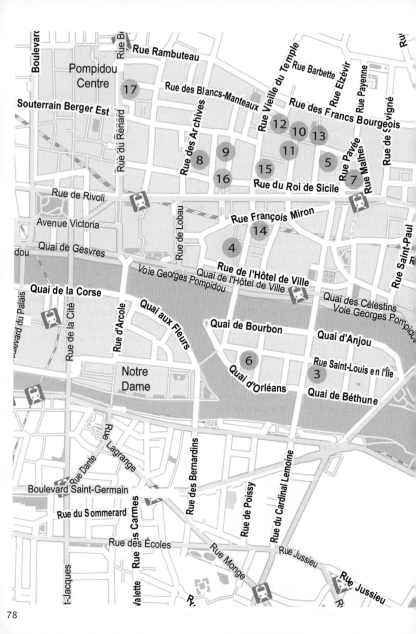

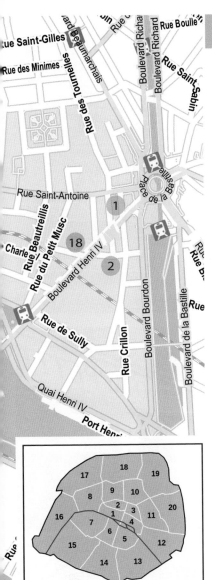

4th Arrondissement

1. Café Ginger
2. Le Grand Appetit
3. Berthillon
4. l'Ebouillanté
5. Kosher Pizza
6. Mon Vieil Ami
7. Pitzman
8. Le Pain Quotidien
9. le Pas-Sage Obligé
10. l'As du Falafel
11. Mi-Va-Mi
12. Chez Hanna
13. King Falafel Palace
14. Chez Izrael
15. Lush Spa, 18 rue du Renard (p.36)
16. Thrift stores (p.36)
17. Bio c'Bon, 26 rue du Renard (p.30)
18. Bio c'Bon, 16 rue de la Cerisaie (p.30)
19. Naturalia, 84 rue Beaubourg (p.31)

- 🟢 100% vegetarian restaurant
- 🟠 restaurant/cafe
- 🟢 shop
- ⚫ hotel/ hostel
- ⚫ cookery school/caterer
- 🟢 local group/ organisation

Le Grand Appetit
Vegan macrobiotic restaurant & shop

- 🖝 9 Rue de la Cerisaie
  Cross street: rue de l'Arsenal
- ☎ 01 40 27 04 95
- ⊖ Métro: Bastille
- 🕓 M–Th 12.00–21.00, F 12.00–
  14.00, Sa–Su closed;
  Closed most of August
- ↘ www.legrandappetit.fr

One of the city's original macrobiotic restaurants is also one of the few that remain fish-free and totally vegan. A vintage '70s vibe permeates both the restaurant and the attached natural foods store next door.

What this place does best are its macro plates, which come in small or large sizes. Expect two kinds of cooked grains, cooked vegetables, seaweed salad, fresh greens, and bread for the table.

You set the table yourself—water, condiments, and cutlery are on a side table—order the food at the counter, and wait.

Sushi rolls, miso soup, and low-sugar desserts are other possibilities.

Credit cards accepted.

Berthillon
Omnivorous café

- 📍 29–31 rue Saint Louis en l'Île
  Cross street: rue des Deux Ponts
- 📞 01 43 54 31 61
- 🚇 Métro: Hôtel de Ville
- 🕐 W–Su 12.00–20.00; Closed
  Mondays and Tuesdays
- 🔗 www.berthillon.fr

The ultimate spot to stop for an icy-cold, deliciously flavorful scoop of sorbet.

Usually, vegans are relegated to the fruit flavors, but at Berthillon, you get to choose among such alluring flavors as Extra Bitter Dark Chocolate, Lemon-Thyme, Whiskey-Chocolate, and Peach with Mint Leaves. Other flavors include Blood Orange, Wild Blackberry, and Rhubarb.

Eat in the tea room, or take your cup or cone to go. Credit cards accepted.

l'Ebouillanté
Omnivorous fusion

- 📍 6 Rue Des Barres
  Cross street: quai de l'Hôtel de Ville
- 📞 01 42 74 70 52
- 🚇 Métro: Pont Marie or Hôtel de Ville
- 🕐 M–Su 12.00–22.00

This darling spot in the thick of Paris's oldest neighborhood offers welcoming respite from sightseeing overload. Chinese teas, homemade lemonade, brick (thin semolina crêpes stuffed with a variety of fillings), and salads hit the spot when hunger strikes.

Let them know if you're vegan and they'll help you find something without cheese or eggs; if you're lucky, they'll make you a crêpe with spinach, mushrooms, and olives.

English spoken and service is super-friendly.

Wine is served in a unique way: Order a bottle, and only pay for what you drink.

Expect generous portions, and if you love the dark stuff, try a rich bowl (yes, bowl) of hot chocolate that has the power to take the edge off of any gray Parisian day.

Kid-friendly. Terrace seating. Dog-friendly. Credit cards accepted.

Kosher Pizza
Omnivorous pizza

- 📍 11 rue des Rosiers
  Cross street: rue Ferdinand Duval
- ☎ 01 48 87 56 88
- ⊖ Métro: Saint-Paul
- ⏱ M-Th 11.00–18.00, Friday 11.00–14.99, and Su 11.00–18.00

All the pizzas in this tiny, six-table rue des Rosiers institution can be made cheese-free, and you even get a 50 centime discount on a single slice, or 2 euros off an entire pie for going sans fromage. Pies boast a thin crust, are 100-percent kosher, and totally tasty. Try the Verdi—onions, peppers, corn, and mushrooms (€16 /15 for to-go orders)—or the Venezia, with grilled eggplant (€13/12).

Kid-friendly. Credit cards accepted.

Mon Vieil Ami
Omnivorous French

- 📍 69 rue Saint Louis en l'Île
  Cross street: rue le Regrattier
- ☎ 01 40 46 01 35
- ⊖ Métro: Pont Marie
- ⏱ M-Su 12.00–14.00 and 19.00–23.00
- ➤ www.mon-vieil-ami.com

Revered by omnivores for both its cuisine and too-perfect location on Île Saint Louis, Mon Vieil Ami is also winning veg converts with its 100 percent légumes (€39) menu that reads like an ode to seasonal vegetables: Asparagus soup; fava bean, pea, and mushroom fricassée; vegetables of the moment served as a tagine with dried apricots and nuts; fresh fruit with mint; and housemade sorbet for dessert.

Vegan options available à la carte or as a complete menu. Worth the splurge, and definitely a special spot for a romantic dinner à deux. Credit cards accepted.

Le Pain Quotidien
Omnivorous healthy

☞ 18-20 Rue des Archives
  Cross street: Rue de Rivoli

☏ 01 44 54 03 07

⊖ Métro: Hôtel de Ville

🕐 M–Su 8.00–20.00

🔗 www.lepainquotidien.com

This Belgian organic-food chain offers a calm, pleasant dining experience, with communal tables, big windows and natural light, and friendly service. Vegan and vegetarian items are plentiful and clearly marked.

Most dishes come with the trademark "pain" (bread) served with a variety of jams and spreads. Tartines (open-faced sandwiches), soups, and salads are filling, if a little on the expensive side.

Organic wine served, as well as juice, coffee, and tea.

Kid-friendly. Credit cards accepted. Other locations in Paris include the 2nd, 9th, and 18th.

le Pas-Sage Obligé
Omnivorous French fusion

☞ 29 rue de Bourg Tibourg
  Cross street: rue de Rivoli

☏ 01 40 41 95 03

⊖ Métro: Hôtel de Ville

🕐 M-F 19.00–22.00, Sa 12.00–14.30 and 19.00–22.30, Su 12.00–14.30 and 19.00–22.00. Closed most of August.

🔗 www.lepassageoblige.com

Great location in the heart of the gay Marais, walking distance to the best bars, shops, and sites the neighborhood has to offer.

Try the mushroom terrine with figs (€5.40), or the refreshing gazpacho (€5.40). For something heartier, there's the seitan-olive burger (€14.90), stuffed pepper (€13.50) and Mushroom roast (€15.80) and strawberry-rhubarb crumble (€6.90) for dessert.

Sunday brunch September-June.

Credit cards accepted. Make a reservation on line if you fear the French phone call.

Pitzman
Omnivorous Israeli

- ☛ 8 rue Pavée
  Cross street: rue de Rivoliî
- ☎ 01 42 71 17 17
- ⊖ Métro: Saint-Paul
- ◐ M–Th and Su 9.00–23.30, F
  9.00–12.00; closed Saturdays

If you feel claustrophobic and don't want to face the crowds on rue des Rosiers, do like the neighborhood locals and head to this standout kosher deli and restaurant offering plenty of cozy seating for a relaxed meal.

The menu is 90-percent veg, and loaded with nibbles like house-made bagels, latkes, strudel, and, of course, falafel (€5). You can also tuck into a filling assiette loaded with hummus, salad, pizza, and other tempting morsels.

Kosher wines, soft drinks, and friendly service. Credit cards accepted.

Chez Izrael
Omnivorous food store

- ☛ 30 Rue François-miron
  Cross street: rue du Pont Louis Philippe
- ☎ 01 42 72 66 23
- ⊖ Métro: St. Paul
- ◐ M–Sa 9:30–19.00; Su closed

A treasure trove of spices, dried fruit and nuts, snacks, liqueurs, candies, olives, and mystery treats from every corner of the globe. A fun place to source unusual souvenirs, and stock up on snacks for long days spent exploring the cobbled streets of Paris. Credit cards accepted.

Rue des Rosiers Falafel Fix
Falafel take-aways

Who comes to the Marais and doesn't get a falafel? No one! Paris's most popular street for partaking in this food-centric ritual is rue des Rosiers. Here, men in tall black hats and long beards mingle among the tourists, giving life to one of the the city's oldest and most picturesque quarters.

The undisputed winner of the falafel contest is l'As du Fallafel (34 rue des Rosiers)—I mean, Lenny Kravitz eats here, for goodness' sake. (And they've got the pictures on the wall to prove it) Eat inside or take your falafel to go for a 2 euro discount. The line moves fast, either way. Inside, you have the option of wine, fries, and other edibles, plus the addictive and oh-so garlicky house-made harissa sauce. Mmmm.

Directly across from l'As is Mi-Va-Mi (23 rue des Rosiers), which churns out equally delicious yet slightly less celebrated falafel, plus fries and Maccabee beer.

Heading west, you'll bump into Chez Hanna (54 rue des Rosiers), where you can enjoy a sit-down falafel feast in a refined setting.

Heading east, you can't miss King Falafel Palace (26 rue des Rosiers), with its outdoor seating and awning to protect diners from the mid-day sun.

In respect of the Jewish Sabbath, these authentic Israeli falafel joints are closed from Friday evening through Saturday. If it's Saturday and you've got to have your falafel, there's always Maoz on the other side of the Seine.

5th Arrondissement

The Latin Quarter is where all the brainpower in Paris congregates. The Sorbonne is here, and the neighborhood caters to students on limited budgets.

Look for bargain bites, bookstores, and several museums, including the Musée National du Moyen Age, with its beautiful tapestries, statues, and Gallo-Roman relics. The Institut du Monde Arabe is also worth a visit, and when you've had enough art and history, there's literature to consider: World famous English-language bookstore Shakespeare and Company offers author readings, music events, and books galore for bookish travelers.

Neighborhood Favorite

Vegan Folie's
Vegan organic bakery

- 🐷 53 rue Mouffetard
  Cross street: rue Ortolan
- ☎ 01 43 37 21 89
- ⊖ Métro: Place Monge
- 🕐 Tu-Su 11.00-20.00; M closed; closed most of August
- ➤ www.veganfolies.fr
  Facebook Vegan Folie's

The city's first and only organic, all-vegan patisserie spot has expanded from its creative sweet and savory cupcakes and sumptuous cheesecakes to include an array of baguette sandwiches: ham, chorizo, and meatless pâté—all vegan, of course!

Friendly service (English spoken), a nice variety of beverages (try the coconut water), and decadent cookies and brownies on offer. A good place to meet up with visiting vegans, and to gather information on local veg events.

Minimum seating, but to-go orders available. Try the whoopee pies and carrot cake too.

Credit cards accepted.

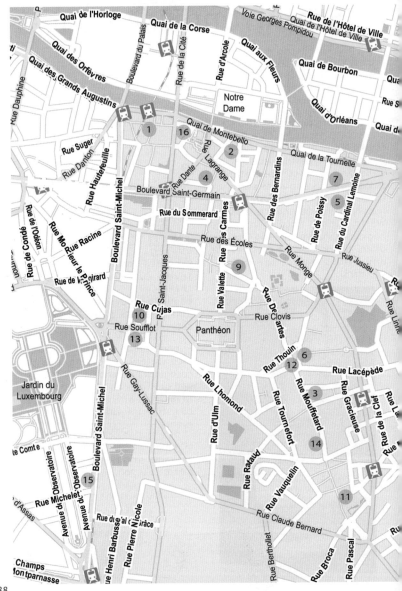

5th Arrondissement

1. Maoz
2. Le Grenier de Notre Dame
3. Vegan Folie's
4. Krishna Bhavan
5. Le Puit de Légumes
6. Cinq Saveurs d'Anada
7. L'Atlas
8. Café de la Grande Mosquée
9. Godjo
10. Tugalik
11. Boca Mexa
12. Chido
13. Biocoop, 1 rue le Goff (p.30)
14. Naturalia, 94 rue Mouffetard (p.31)
15. Nouveaux Robinson, 78 bd St Michel (p.31)
16. Shakespeare & Co. English bookshop,
    37 Rue de la Bûcherie

- 100% vegetarian restaurant
- restaurant/cafe
- shop
- hotel/ hostel
- cookery school/caterer
- local group/ organisation

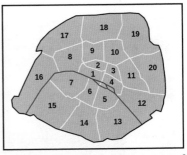

Maoz (5th)
Vegan falafel cafe & takeaway

- ☛ 8 rue Xavier Privas
  Cross street: Quai Saint-Michel
- ☏ 01 43 26 36 00
- ⊖ Métro: Saint-Michel
- ◕ Su-W 11.00-23:00, Th-Sa
  11.00-02.00

The original vegan fast-food joint is still a contender for Best Falafel in Paris. Generous portions, an all-you-can salad-and-sauces station, drinks, and very limited seating are what you'll find at this corner hole-in-the-wall. Add fries and a few generous squirts from the hummus pump and you'll be stuffed until midnight.

The standard formule (€8) includes a falafel sandwich, fries, and a soft drink; falafel sandwich à la carte will set you back less than €5. Cash only.

Can be hard to find in a tangled maze of tourist-trap eateries; try to enter from Quai Saint-Michel for easy spotting. If no seats are available, relish your meal in the park beside Notre Dame or nearby square Viviani. Another branch in the 6th (pg. 97).

Le Grenier de Notre Dame
French vegetarian restaurant

- ☛ 18 rue de la Bûcherie
  Cross street: rue Dante
- ☏ 01 43 29 98 29
- ⊖ Métro: Saint-Michel
- ◕ M-Th and Su 12:00-14.30 and
  18.30-22.30, F-Sa 12:00-14.00
  and 18.30-23.00
- ☈ www.legrenierdenotredame.com

Darling spot with terrace seating, and two floors of indoor dining. Service is efficient and the meals are filling.

Couscous, macrobiotic dishes, lots of seitan and tofu options, and interesting salads. Good selection of vegan options, and some gluten-free.

Mid-day formule is €15.50; evening and weekends €17.50. Look for veg versions of traditional French classics like cassoulet and tartare d'avocat, but if you're really hungry, go for the escalope de seitan.

The drinks menu features wine, smoothies, coffee and tea.

Terrace seating. Credit cards accepted.

Krishna Bhavan
Vegetarian Indian restaurant

- 25 rue Galande
  Cross street: rue Dante
- 01 43 29 87 93
- Métro: Maubert-Mutualité
- M–Su 12.00–23.00

Just a block away from Notre Dame and Paris's most popular indie bookstore, Shakespeare & Co., Krishna Bhavan offers cheap, tasty Indian and Sri Lankan meals that are 100-percent vegetarian.

Thalis (€10), dosas, idli, and treats like aloo paratha and chole bhatura can all be found on the extensive menu.

Menus (€14.50 lunch/€19.00 dinner) include a starter (samosa, vada, soup) main plat (rice and curried veg), dessert, and a drink.

Wine and soft drinks, plus traditional chai and non-vegan lassis.

Terrace seating. Kid-friendly. Credit cards accepted.

Also in the 10th, pg. 133.

Le Puit de Légumes
Vegetarian and fish restaurant

- 18 rue Cardinal Lemoine
  Cross street: blvd Saint-Germain
- 01 43 25 50 95
- Métro: Cardinal Lemoine
- M–Sa 12:00–16:00 and 19:00–22:00; closed Sundays
- www.lepuitsdelegumesbio.fr

Cozy and cute, and a bit like stepping back in time a few decades, this "vegetarian" restaurant serves fish, but almost anything can be veganized and everything offered has a vegetarian base.

Several different lunch formules to choose from, including the Zen meal (€15) served with miso soup; a macro plate with grains, tofu, and greens; and vanilla soy cream for dessert.

The à la carte menu includes savory tarts, salads, tofu plates, soups, and low-sugar desserts.

Wine, juices, and herbal infusions feature on the drinks menu. Pet-friendly. Credit cards accepted.

Cinq Saveurs d'Anada
Vegetarian and fish restaurant

- 72 rue du Cardinal Lemoine
  cross street: rue Rollin
- Métro: Cardinal Lemoine
- T–Su 11.00–14.30 and 19.00–22.30
- www.anada-5-saveurs.com

The beautiful, filling plats are the thing to order at this 90-percent vegetarian restaurant. Colorful, bountiful salads, a side of grains and cooked veggies, plus either tofu, seitan, or tempeh (€15.90) makes a filling, healthy lunch.

Other possibilities include the soup du jour (€7.20); giant composed salad (€11.80); or a hearty full menu (€29.90) that includes soup, main plate with seitan or tempeh, grains and veggies, dessert, and coffee or tea.

Lots of dessert options for vegans, including apple crumble with nuts (€6.50).

Coffee with rice milk (€3.20), Japanese green teas (€3.20), and wine by the glass or bottle are among the drinks options. Credit cards accepted .

L'Atlas
Omnivorous North African restaurant

- 12 blvd Saint-Germain
  Cross street: rue du Cardinal Lemoine
- 01 44 07 23 66
- Métro: Maubert Mutualité or Cardinal Lemoine
- W–Su 12:30–14.30 and 19.30–23.00; Tu 19.30–23.00; closed Mondays
- www.latlas.fr

This charming corner spot offers sumptuous Moroccan ambience and the chance to try a variety of North African dishes.

Start with the startlingly tasty eggplant-artichoke salad (€9) or the heftier Moroccan "special" salad (€12), and then go for the couscous légumes (€19) with chickpeas, carrot, potato, and dried fruit.

Plenty of dessert options for vegans, including the intriguing fig-and-date sorbet (€10).

Fruit juices, beer, and Moroccan wine are served, as well as the house specialty, tea with pine nuts! Kid-friendly. Credit cards accepted.

Café de la Grande Mosquée
Omnivorious North African

- 39 Rue Geoffroy Saint-Hilaire
  Cross street: rue Daubenton
- 01 43 31 38 20
- Métro: Place Monge
- M–Su 9.00–00.00
- www.la-mosquee.com

If a mosque seems like an unusual spot for an afternoon pick-me-up, well, that's because it is. Wonderfully unusual, in that you can sip mint tea (€2) and nibble on sticky pastries (€2) at the mosque's pleasant cafe, and even get a massage at the on-site hammam.

Stepping into the café's beautiful, mosaic-tiled interior feels like you've entered an authentic Moroccan souk; cool and shady, with a distinctly non-Parisian flavor.

The attached restaurant offers couscous végétarienne, several egg- and dairy-free salads, and that Paris restaurant staple, French fries.

Terrace seating. Credit cards accepted.

Godjo
Omnivorous Ethiopian

☛ 8 Rue de l'École Polytechnique
Cross street: rue des Ecoles

☏ 01 40 46 82 21

⊖ Métro: Maubert Mutualité

◕ M 19.00–23.30, Tu–Su 12.00–
15.00 and 19.00–23.30

↖ www.godjo.com

The subterranean dining room is popular with groups, and the food at Godjo is popular with everyone who eats here.

Fresh and tasty vegetarian platter (€15) goes best when washed down with a bottle of St. George Ethiopian beer, but you can also order each of the six vegetarian options separately. Gamen Wot (spinach) is always perfectly spiced, and the Messer (lentils) can be prepared either hot or mild (€11.50).

Wine and soft drinks served; more expensive than other Ethiopian places in town and the service can be spotty, but the neighborhood is great and the food authentic and warming. Credit cards accepted.

Tugalik
Ominivorous macrobiotic–French

☛ 4 Rue Toullier
Cross street: rue Soufflot

☏ 01 43 54 41 49

⊖ Métro: Cluny La Sorbonne or Cardinal Lemoine

◕ M 11.30–14.30; Tu–F 11.30–22.30; Sa 19.00–22.30; closed Sundays

↖ www.tugalik.com

The menu changes every week at this healthy, elegant French macro–style restaurant.

Creamy risotto with root vegetables (€18), almond–leek terrine with truffle oil (€11) and enormous organic salads with warm grains (€8.50), and gluten-free carrot cake (€8) are some of the tempting vegan options.

Special vegetarian dinners with wine pairing (€45) are another reason to dine here.

Menus past have included pumpkin ravioli with mushroom cream; buckwheat crepes with winter vegetables; and braised vegetables atop polenta cake with orange reduction sauce.

Organic wines by the bottle and the glass. Credit cards accepted.

Also in the 6th, pg. 102.

Burrito Sandwich on rue Mouffetard

- www.bocamexa.com
- www.chido.fr

Rue Mouffetard has lots of appeal; it's a cute shopping street lined with cafes, bars, and interesting shops (some tourist traps, but not all), a subterranean bowling alley, theaters, and a giant Naturalia supermarket.

On Sundays, an accordionist plays at Place de la Contrescarpe, and out of the cobbled corners drift in the dancers, who evoke another era with their dancing à deux.

Mouffetard is also home to Paris's only vegan cupcake and pastry shop, Vegan Folie's. But before you dig into your thick slice of dairy-free peanut-butter chocolate cheesecake, you need lunch.

For a quick, cheap, and filling meal-on-the-go, hit up one of the burrito spots that vie for your business on this little sliver of a street. At the foot of the hill sits Boca Mexa (127 rue Mouffetard, daily 10.00-22.00, F-Sa till 23.00) where you can get yourself a meat-free burrito, quesadilla, tacos, or even nachos, and wash it down with a refreshing agua fresco. At the top of the hill, Chido (3 rue Mouffetard, daily 11.30-23.30, F-Sa till 01.00) proposes burritos, salads, guacamole, and margaritas. Olé!

6th Arrondissement

The 6th was the center of Paris's Left-Bank literary scene back in the early part of the 20th century. Hemingway, Baldwin, Joyce, Stein, and Fitzgerald mingled with the likes of Picasso and Modigliani at Les Deux Magots, Café Flore, and Brasserie Lipp—cafés that still exist today—creating art and making history.

In the 21st century, the 6th is known more for its famous park, Luxembourg Gardens, than anything else. However, there's lots to do here, including catching a show at one of dozens of independent movie houses, and visiting the prestigious Ecole des Beaux Arts, where you can see the work of up and coming artists as well as established names in the art world.

While the classic cafés aren't the most veg-friendly spots in Paris, you can still take a seat on the terrace and enjoy your €7 café with a chic vantage point.

Local favorite

Maoz (6th)
Vegan falafel

☛ 36 Rue Saint-André des Arts
 Cross street: rue Séguier
⊖ Métro: St. Michel or Odéon
◐ Su-W 11.00-23.00,
 Th-Sa 11.00-02.00

Late weekend hours make this a great post-nighclub nosh spot.

Different from its sister location a short walk away in the 5th (pg.90), this Maoz branch offers couscous with vegetables along with the standard falafel, fries, and all-you-can-eat salad-and-pickles bar.

The Maoz menu (€7.95) includes a falafel sandwich, fries, and drink.

The Falafel salad formule (bowl of salad with three falafel, plus all you can eat from the bar) plus drink is good value (€5.95) for those on a budget.

Fries and a variety of soft drinks available.

Limited seating. Cash only

6th Arrondissement

1. Maoz 2
2. Guen Mai
3. Pizza Chic
4. Tch'a
5. Le Petit Jacob
6. Tugalik
7. Holy Planet
8. Les Nouveaux Robinson,
   78 bd St Michel (p.31)
9. Bio Génération,
   68-70 rue du Cherche-Midi (p.31)

- 100% vegetarian restaurant
- restaurant/cafe
- shop
- hotel/ hostel
- cookery school/caterer
- local group/ organisation

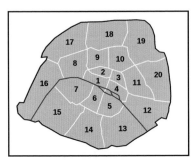

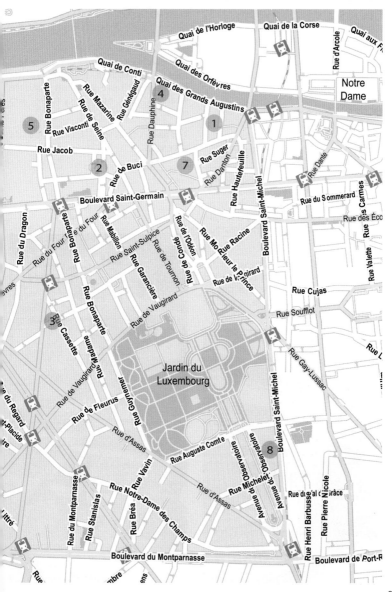

Guen Mai
Macrobiotic vegan & fish restaurant
and health food store

- 🠶 6 rue Cardinale
  Cross street: rue de l'Abbaye
- ☎ 01 43 26 03 24
- ⊖ Métro: Saint-Germain des Prés
  or Mabillon
- ◑ Restaurant M–Sa 12.00–15.30;
  Shop M–Sa 09.30–22.30;
  Su closed

The menu at this natural-food store/
café is 80 percent vegan, and mostly
macrobiotic. Everything on the menu
tastes really fresh, and the prices are
more reasonable than other restaurants of the macro ilk.

Quinoa burgers, Vietnamese spring
rolls, ravioli, and seitan brochettes
are among the many delicious possibilities that can be ordered as part of
a formule (€12.50) or à la carte.

Fresh-pressed juices (€5) and simple,
house-made desserts round out the
menu.

When you've polished off every last
morsel on your plate, browse the
boutique, where you can procure
vitamins, teas, non-dairy milks, and
other veg supplies.

Terrace seating. Credit cards
accepted.

Le Petit Jacob
Omnivorous organic wine & tapas bar

- 40 rue Jacob
  Cross street: rue Bonaparte
- 06 25 84 33 15
- Métro: Saint-Germain-des-Pres
- M–Sa 12.00–15.00 and 19.00–00.00; closed Sundays

An organic wine bar where you can fill your stomach with a variety of interesting small plates, then souse yourself in organic wines by the glass or bottle (starting at €3.50).

Ask the host what goes best with organic lentils with roasted artichoke (€8), and she'll happily advise. Soups (€4.50), salads (€7.50–9.50), and tartines (open-faced sandwiches) round out the veg possibilities.

A cozy place to escape the rain and sate yourself on a gray Paris afternoon. Pet-friendly. Credit cards accepted.

Pizza Chic
Omnivorous Italian

- 13 Rue de Mézières
  Cross street: rue de Rennes
- 01 45 48 30 38
- Métro: Saint-Sulpice
- M–Th 12.30–14.30 and 19.30–23.00; F 12.30–14.30 and 19.30–23.30; Sa 12.30–15.00 and 19.30–23.00, Su 12.00–15.00 and 19.30–22.00
- www.pizzachic.fr

There are regular ol' pizza places and then there are fancy pizza places, and Pizza Chic definitely falls into the latter category. Cloth napkins, über-professional wait service, and stylish décor makes dining here a truly pleasurable experience.

Starters include chestnut soup with truffles (€12) and the simple but tasty garden salad (€10).

The chef will happily prepare any of their gorgeous pizzas (€14–22) sans fromage (without cheese); try the artichoke pizza for something completely different.

The craziest dessert item on the menu—a slushy made with lemon sorbet, vodka, and sparkling prosecco wine (€10)—is accidentally vegan, and guaranteed to put you in a good mood.

Credit cards accepted.

Tch'a
Omnivorous Tea House

- 6 rue du Pont-de-Lodi
  Cross street: Quai des Grands Augustins
- 01 43 29 61 31
- Métro: Mabillon or Saint-Michel
- Tu-Sa 12.00-19.00 (tea service only after 15.00); Su 12.00-16.00; closed Mondays

Tofu and tea are at the heart of this menu. Step in and unwind over a fragrant bowl of lapsong suchong poured from a diminutive pot, and dig into a plateful of fresh tofu and expertly cooked veggies. Won-ton soup, Sichuan tofu, and bowls of perfectly cooked rice make this sweet spot hidden in the Latin Quarter worth seeking out. Credit cards accepted.

Tugalik
Omnivorous French

- 29 rue Saint-Placide
  Cross street: Raspail
- 01 42 84 02 04
- Métro: Rennes or Saint-Placide
- M-Sa 10.00-20.00, Su closed. Closed most of August.

Unlike its sister restaurant in the neighboring 5th (pg. 94), this Tugalik outpost isn't open for dinner, but its menu still offers all of the organic deliciousness and bright flavors of the other location.

Chickpea crepe with coriander chutney, quinoa salad with vegetables, and pumpkin soup with coconut milk are some of the items you might find on the menu that changes weekly.

Organic wines, vegan desserts, and lots of gluten-free options. Credit cards accepted.

Holy Planet
Vegetarian natural foods store

- 34 rue Serpente
  Cross street: rue Danton
- 01 42 97 53 24
- Métro: Odéon
- M-Sa 11.00-20.00, Sun closed

Part natural-foods store, part organic vegetarian takeaway shop, Holy Nature offers a good selection of vegan to-go items, including soup, a salad bar with 15 different ingredients, and sandwiches made with vegan pâtés, veggies, and fake meats.

Fresh fruit juices and a super-friendly, helpful staff await. A few seats available inside.

Wine and beer for sale. Credit cards accepted.

7th Arrondissement

Everyone who passes through Paris visits the 7th at some point, if only to stop and gaze up at the city's most celebrated monument, the Tour Eiffel.

This district is also home to Napoleon's Tomb, the Assemblée Nationale, Rodin museum and gardens, and the always-amazing Musée d'Orsay.

The American Library is another must-visit; on Wednesday nights, the library hosts author events and lectures, complete with wine and snacks. It's one of the best places for meeting local Anglophones, but if you prefer to mingle with a more local crowd, veer away from the famous landmark and explore the quiet back-streets of the 7th.

Veggie
Vegetarian French

- ☛ 38 rue de Verneuil
  Cross street: rue du Bac
- ☎ 01 42 61 28 61
- ⊖ Métro: rue du Bac or Solferino
- ◑ M–F 9.30–15.00 and 17.00–19.00; Sa–Su closed

Within walking distance of the Musée d'Orsay, this tiny, totally organic lunch and early dinner spot offers predictably tasty menu items for hungry herbivores: Vegetable tarts, soups, salads, desserts. Expect to spend about €15 on lunch.

Wine, fresh fruit juices, and takeaway option. Credit cards accepted.

Little-known fact:
The Tour Eiffel is not vegan!
We're not talking about the celebrated *Jules Verne* (2nd floor) nor the *58 Tour Eiffel* (1st floor) restaurants in the Eiffel Tower — which are clearly not vegan (though they do propose vegetarian options); we're talking about the tower itself! The elevators are still greased in the same way they were when it was completed in 1889: with *graisse de boeuf*, aka beef fat.

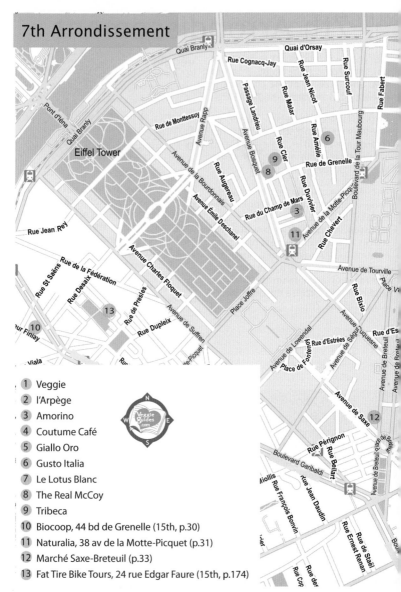

7th Arrondissement

1 Veggie
2 l'Arpège
3 Amorino
4 Coutume Café
5 Giallo Oro
6 Gusto Italia
7 Le Lotus Blanc
8 The Real McCoy
9 Tribeca
10 Biocoop, 44 bd de Grenelle (15th, p.30)
11 Naturalia, 38 av de la Motte-Picquet (p.31)
12 Marché Saxe-Breteuil (p.33)
13 Fat Tire Bike Tours, 24 rue Edgar Faure (15th, p.174)

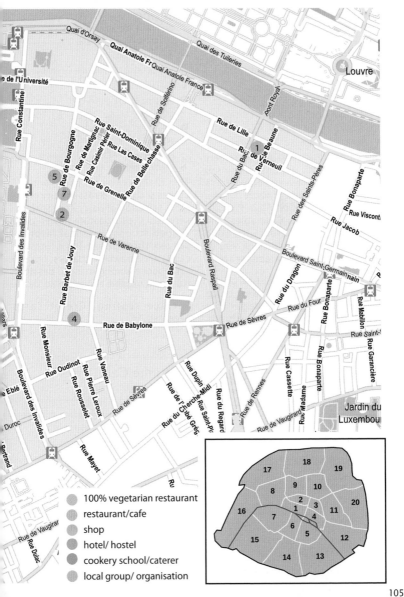

100% vegetarian restaurant
restaurant/cafe
shop
hotel/ hostel
cookery school/caterer
local group/ organisation

l'Arpège
Omnivorous French

- 84 rue de Varenne
  Cross street: rue de Bourgogne
- 01 45 50 23 16
- Métro: Varenne
- M-F 12.00–14.00 and 19.00–22.30; Sa–Su closed
- www.alain-passard.com

This world-renowned and extremely exclusive (read: expensive) dining spot should be every vegetarian's entrée into the world of haute cuisine. Michelin-starred chef Alain Passard is passionate about vegetables, and each dish is prepared with such expert skill that you'll think you've died and gone to vegetable heaven.

The tasting menu is full of surprises. One day, you might find sweet onion gratin with truffles, vegetable dumplings floating in a savory broth, an exquisite piece of turnip *nigiri*, or a *merguez* sausage fashioned out of vegetables.

Reservations a must, and expect to drop hundreds of euro for the experience. Credit cards accepted.

Amorino
Omnivorous ice-cream

- 42 rue Cler
  Cross street: rue de Grenelle
- 09 50 79 33 93
- Métro: École Militaire
- Mar–Oct M–Su 12.00–22.30 and 24.00 at weekends; winter closes 21.30; Jan–Feb closes 19.30.
- www.amorino.com/en

This chain ice-cream parlor with 25 outlets scattered across the city offers a big selection of dairy-free sorbets, served in their signature flower-petal shaped scoops. Seasonal favorites served throughout Paris include cassis and strawberry flavors, but you can choose among mango, passion-fruit, and organic chocolate sorbetto.

Terrace seating. Credit cards accepted.

Coutume Café
Omnivorous fusion

- 47 rue de Babylone
  Cross street: rue Vaneau
- 01 45 51 50 47
- Métro: Saint-François-Xavier
- M-F 8.30–19.00; Sa–Su 10.00–19.00
- www.facebook.com/Coutume

Run by a Franco-Australian duo, this is the spot in Paris to get a caffeine-infused liquid elixir, and fill up on tasty light meals and sturdier weekend brunch.

Salads and pasta dishes make the best bets for vegans; vegetarians can expand their horizons to include a simple breakfast (€7) of juice, coffee and either pancakes or viennoisserie. The lunch special (€13) might include carrot soup, buckwheat noodles with lotus root and vegetables, and a coffee of your choice.

A stylish, trendy spot to hang out and get wired. Artisan beer, iced drinks, and soy milk available on occasion.

Free wifi. Credit cards accepted.

Giallo Oro
Omnivorous Italian

- ☛ 38 rue de Bourgogne
  Cross street: rue de Grenelle
- ☎ 01 45 50 14 57
- ⊖ Métro: Varenne
- ◕ M-Sa 12.00-14.30 and 19.00-23.00

The aromas wafting out of the kitchen should be enough to seduce any diner, but the huge selection of vegetarian dishes—pasta is the specialty here—is the main draw.

Risotto with fresh asparagus, porcini gnocchi (€18), mustard-greens ravioli (€15), and another delicious rendition of pasta primavera (€15) are just a few of the carb-lover's specials on the menu.

Wine by the glass or bottle, mixed drinks, and friendly service await. Credit cards accepted.

Gusto Italia
Omnivorous Italian

- ☛ 11 rue Amelie
  Cross street: rue Saint-Dominique
- ☎ 01 45 56 92 70
- ⊖ Métro: La Tour-Maubourg or Invalides
- ◕ M-Su 12.00-23.00

Tucked on a side street between rue de Grenelle and lively shopping street rue Saint-Dominique, you'll find the adorable, closet-sized pizzeria Gusto Italia. No frills, but the pizzas (€9-14) are tasty and every pie can be made cheese-free on request.

Try the tasty trifecta of grilled veg pizza (€9), mixed salad (€9), and verre de vin rouge (red wine).

Filling lasagna and pasta dishes are other possibilities, both here and at the two nearby Gusto Italia locations on rue de Grenelle. Credit cards accepted.

Le Lotus Blanc
Omnivorous Vietnamese

- ☛ 45 rue de Bourgogne
  Cross street: rue de Varenne
- ☎ 01 45 55 18 89
- ⊖ Métro: Varenne
- ◕ M-F 12.00-14.30 and M-Sa 19.30-23.00

A five-minute walk from the Rodin museum and 10 minutes from Invalides, this adorable, authentic Vietnamese restaurant has more

This "American café" fills a certain void—one that calls for peanut-butter on bagel (€3.50) and nachos with guacamole (€6). Salads (€7) and gringo-style super burritos (€6) are other affordable possibilities.

American junk food (Oreos, Reese's Peanut Butter Cups) and canned goods (black beans, jalapeno peppers) are for sale in the general store section. Credit cards accepted.

going for it than just its great location.

A vegetarian menu includes such scrumptious treats as tofu-vermicelli soup (€8.50), vegetarian duck with mushroom and bamboo (€12.80), and tofu with lemongrass (€11.80).

The set menu (€22.90) includes an entrée, main plate with rice, dessert and coffee.

The main dining room looks small—and it is—but there's more seating upstairs. Credit cards accepted.

The Real McCoy/McCoy Café
Omnivorous American

- 194 rue de Grenelle
  Cross street: ave Bosquet
- 01 45 56 00 00
- Métro: École Militaire
- M–Su 10.00–20.00;
  closed most of August

Tribeca
Omnivorous Italian

- 36 rue Cler
  Cross street: rue de Grenelle
- 01 45 55 12 01
- Métro: École Militaire
- M–Sa 8:30–23.45, Su 11.00–17.00

Pedestrian street rue Cler has a cult following among tourists, but locals alike love this Italian spot with the giant terrace and huge menu loaded with veg options.

All pizzas (€9–12) are prepared fresh and can be made cheeseless, Rigatoni with truffles (€13), vegetable lasagna (€9), and a lots of veg entrees (€7–10) to keep you full and happy until Eiffel Tower twinkle time.

Kid-friendly. Terrace seating. Dog-friendly. Credit cards accepted.

8th Arrondissement

Like the neighboring 9th, Paris's 8th arrondissement is a financial district buzzing with men and women in suits who pour out of their Haussmann offices several times a day to smoke en masse on the broad sidewalks.

The Champs Elysées is the neighborhood's big draw; here you'll find the famous topless cabaret, the Lido, plus several theaters, cinemas, and shopping complexes.

Skip the overpriced cafés lining the famous 10-lane thoroughfare and opt for something on a side street that's quieter and friendlier on the wallet.

Bert's
Omnivorous café

☛ 4 Avenue du Président Wilson
Cross street: Georges V
☏ 01 47 23 48 37
⊖ Métro: Alma-Marceau
🕐 M–F 8.00–20.30, Sa–Su 9.30–20.30
↖ www.berts.fr

Across from the Princess Diana memorial and a five minute walk to the Palais de Tokyo, Musée Galleria, and the City of Paris's Modern Art Museum, Bert's offers two veg salads per day (€6.90–7.50), two meat-free toasted sandwiches that can be veganized (€6.50), plus a vegan soupe du jour (€4.30).

On lucky days, you might find a veg pasta or tart special on the menu.

If you're feeling fancy, spring for a bottle of champagne (€30–50), or just stick with the invigorating coffee drinks.

Terrace seating. Kid-friendly. Free wifi. Credit cards accepted.

8th Arrondissement

1. Bert's
2. Bio Sphere Café
3. Bread and Roses

Cojean:

4. 55 ave Franklin D Roosevelt
5. 32 rue Monceau
6. 11 ave Delcassé
7. 64 rue Mathurins
8. 19 rue Clément Marot
9. 10 rue de Surène
10. Eat Me
11. L'Envue
12. Matsuri
13. Maison Blanche
14. Le Petit Trend Black
15. Quality & Co.
16. Monoprix
17. La Vie Claire,
    85 boulevard Haussman (p.31)

● 100% vegetarian restaurant
● restaurant/cafe
● shop

111

Bio Sphère Café
Omnivorous gluten-free cafe

- ☛ 47 rue de Laborde
  Cross street: rue de Rocher
- ☎ 01 42 93 45 58
- ⊖ Métro: Europe
- 🕐 Tu-Sa 11.00–17.00, Su-M closed
- ➤ www.biospherecafe.fr/en
  bio-sphere-cafe.blogspot.fr

Quiche, baguette sandwiches, and savory tarts are the cornerstones of every French café's lunch menu, and that's no different at Bio Sphère—except that everything on offer at this modern eatery is gluten-free and organic—including the beer.

Fresh-pressed juices (€4.20) are another house specialty, and they almost help balance out any overindulging that might occur after viewing the patisserie case.

On the savory side, there's soup (€4.70–6.70), Breton galettes (€6.70–11.70), pizzas (€10.79) served with a side salad, and pasta (€10.70).

Credit cards accepted.

Bread and Roses
Omnivorous French

- ☛ 25 rue Boissy d'Anglas
  Cross street: Faubourg Saint-Honoré
- ☎ 01 47 42 40 00
- ⊖ Métro: Concorde
- 🕐 M-F 8.00–20.30; Sa 10.00–20.30; closed Sundays
- ➤ www.breadandroses.fr

Plenty of choices for the vegetarian traveler here, especially if eggs and dairy are part of your diet. Vegans can choose from a variety of salads (which can be prepared without meat or fish), breads, and daily soups.

Try the Tarte Provençale with dried fig, artichokes, and zucchini. Pumpkin soup (€18.50) is served with delicious, fresh bread.

Prices are high here, but you're paying in part for location; just steps away from the Palais Elysées and Paris's high-end shopping street, rue Saint-Honoré, which means you might find yourself dining beside politicians or celebrity types.

Terrace seating. Credit cards accepted.

Cojean
Omnivorous healthy

- 55 ave Franklin D. Roosevelt
  Cross street: Champs Elysées
- 01 45 63 19 09
- Métro: Franklin D. Roosevelt
- M–F 9.00–16.00, Sa–Su closed
- www.cojean.fr

Paris's 8th arrondissement gets to claim the honor of Most Cojean Outlets in a Single Arrondissement (there are six). Whichever spot you happen to visit, look for wheatgrass juice (€3.50), toasted vegetable sandwiches (€4.90), lasagna (€8.90), tasty vegan soups (€4.50–4.90), and salads galore (€2.90–5.90).

Also look for organic juices, bubble tea, and dairy-free tapioca desserts (€2.90).

Cojean caters to the lunchtime office crowd, and both hours and ambience reflect that. Free wifi. Credit cards accepted. Also in the 8th at

    32 rue Monceau
    11 ave Delcassé
    64 rue Mathurins
    19 rue Clément Marot
    11 rue de Surène

Eat Me
Omnivorous healthy

- 35 rue de Washington
  Cross street: Champs Elysées
- 01 40 74 04 44
- Métro: Georges V
- M–F 11.00–15.00; closed
  Saturdays and Sundays
- www.eatme.fr

This four-restaurant Parisian chain offer a variety of salads (quinoa, sesame-tofu), cheesy pastas (€5.50), soups (€3.70) and sandwiches (€4.90–5.40) in a fast-casual, clean and modern environment.

Fresh juices, plus tea, coffee, and soft drinks. Credit cards accepted.

L'Envue
Omnivorous fusion

- 🖝 39 rue Boissy d'Anglas
  Cross street: rue du Faubourg
  Saint-Honoré
- ☎ 01 42 65 10 49
- ⊖ Métro: Madeleine or Concorde
- 🕐 Tu-Sa 08.00–00.00 and M
  08.00–22.00; closed Sundays
- ↖ www.lenvue.com

The owner's wife is a vegetarian, and her influence permeates the menu at this chic, welcoming spot just off of Paris's most exclusive shopping street.

Pastilla with tofu and vegetables is the standout item (€19.50), but the Minceur salad—with rice, asparagus, grapefruit, and tofu (€18)—is worth a taste, too. Risotto, lasagna, and noodles dishes available.

Small plates (€6) include baked endive, stir-fried seasonal veggies, ratatouille, seasonal veg purée, and that perennial favorite, French fries.

Beer, wines by the glass or bottle, classic cocktails, and soft drinks available, and even more vegetarian options available at the upstairs tearoom. Terrace seating. Credit cards accepted.

Matsuri
Omnivorous Japanese

- 🖝 24 rue Marbeuf
  Cross Street: Champs Elysées
- ☎ 01 45 62 30 14
- ⊖ Métro: Franklin D. Roosevelt
- 🕐 M-Sa 12.00–15.00 and 19.00–
  23.00; Su closed
- ↖ www.matsuri.fr

Tucked into a calm courtyard a five-minute walk from the heart of the Champs-Elysées, this calm, cool oasis offers plenty of veg-friendly options.

Favorites include the wakame salad (€4), cucumber maki (€3 for 6 pieces), avocado maki (4.50 for 6 pieces), edamame (€4), and daily specials that might include lotus root-and-tofu salad.

Wine (€3-4 per glass), sake (€12-15 per bottle), green tea, and non-alcoholic drinks are also served. Credit cards accepted.

Matsuri is a chain; another location can be found in the 8th on rue Boètie, as well as in the 16th, and in the La Défense shopping center.

Maison Blanche
Omnivorous fusion

- 15 ave Montaigne
  Cross street: rue du Boccador
- 01 47 23 55 99
- Métro: Alma-Marceau
- M-F 12.00–14.00 and 20.00–23.00; Sa-Su 20.00–23.00
- www.maison-blanche.fr

Upscale dining with lots of veg options—more if you call in advance to make a veg request. Daily formules (€48–110) offer a multi-course gustatory experience. Seasonal vegetables and imaginative flavor pairings make this a special dining experience.

If you're lucky, you'll get to try the gnocchi à la romaine with caramelized sweet onions, or the in-season multi-colored tomatoes drizzled with an exceptionally fruity olive oil from Provence.

After you dine, window shop at some of the most exclusive fashion houses in the world that line this street. Beware: Fur coats (and the people who wear them) abound in this corner of Paris.

Reservations highly recommended at this see-and-be-seen spot. Terrace seating. Credit cards accepted.

Le Petit Trend Black
Omnivorous healthy

- 43 rue Boissy d'Anglas
  Cross street: rue du Faubourg Saint-Honoré
- 01 40 07 58 90
- Métro: Madeleine or Concorde
- M-F 8.30–16.30; closed Saturdays and Sundays
- www.trendblack.com

Sleek, upscale café and sandwich shop with a solid selection of vegan and vegetarian options for big spenders.

In the refrigerator case, you can choose among the regular vegan options: quinoa salad (€6.90) and lentil salad (€6.90), or a big garden salad (€8.20).

Sandwiches can be made meat- and dairy free on request, and the soupe du jour is often vegan.

Very friendly staff. Terrace seating. Free wifi. Credit cards accepted.

Quality & Co. (8th)
Omnivorous healthy

- 37 rue de Berri
  Cross street: Haussmann
- 01 40 74 00 74
- Métro: Saint-Philippe-du-Roule
- M–Sa 8.30–17.00
- www.qualiteandco.com

Like its sister location in the 2nd (pg. 65), the communal tables at this lunchspot give off a school cantine vibe—in the best possible way.

Three vegetarian sandwiches (€4.90–6.80), several vegan soups (€4.30), plus risotto and lasagnas feature on the daily menu. Try the Sexy Rabbit (carrot and ginger) or the quinoa and veggies for something on the lighter end of the spectrum, or one of the toasted veg sandwiches for something a bit more substantial. Free Wifi.

Monoprix
Omnivorous store

- 52–60 Champs Elysées
  Cross street: rue la Boètie
- 01 53 77 65 65
- Métro: Franklin D. Roosevelt or Georges V
- M–Sa 9.00–00.00, Su closed
- www.monoprix.fr

Visiting Monoprix is a must at least once on your trip to Paris, and this giant store on the Champs Elysées is one of the best in the city. Divided into two sections—department store and grocery store—you'll find everything you could possibly need here, from souvenirs and afternoon snacks to new stockings or a beach umbrella.

In the grocery store (entrance on rue la Boètie), look for a huge selection of prefab veg(an) salads—carrot, beet, tabouli, lentils—some of it organic, too. Breads, fresh produce, tofu, vegan pâté, and chocolate bars are among the many edible treats you'll find here. Credit cards accepted.

9th Arrondissement

If you came to Paris to spend your hard-earned cash on clothes, perfume, and baubles, the 9th is your arrondissement. This is grands magasins (department stores) territory: Printemps, Galleries Lafayette, and Citadium shopping complex are all here, as are fast-fashion retails Zara, Uniqlo, H & M, C & A, and Mango.

When you tire of the cha-ching of the cash register, head over to the celebrated Palais Garnier opera house for a culture fix. Whether you pop in for a ballet performance or simply to gaze skyward at the Chagall works beautifying the ceiling, the landmark building is worth a stop.

Nearby is the famed Olympia auditorium, where everyone from the Beatles to the Beastie Boys have performed. Many other live performance venues, big and small, can be found in every corner of the 9th.

Neighborhood favorite

VégéBowl
Vegetarian Asian

- ☛ 3 rue de la Boule Rouge
  Cross street: rue Richer
- ☎ 01 42 46 45 89
- ⊖ Métro: Grands Boulevards
- 🕐 M–F 12.00–14.30 and 19.00–22.30; Sa–Su 19.00–22.30
- 🔖 www.vegebowl.com
  Facebook Vegebowl

Cheerful little place with an incredible 90 percent vegan menu that fuses Vietnamese and Chinese cuisine.

Heavy on the fake-meat dishes, including "beef" brochettes, "chicken" clay pots, and lacquered "duck." Steamed dumplings, taro cakes, soups, salads, and oodles of noodle and rice dishes round out the menu. There's almost too much choice—in the best possible way.

The lunch formule (€12) includes an entrée, plat, and dessert.

Unlike some Asian vegetarian restaurants in Paris, wine is sold here, by the glass, pitcher, and bottle.

Service is friendly, and the ambience is casual but not at all fast-food like. A great place to relax and enjoy a veg meal in pleasant surroundings. Credit cards accepted.

9th Arrondissement

- 100% vegetarian restaurant
- restaurant/cafe
- shop
- hotel/ hostel
- cookery school/caterer
- local group/ organisation

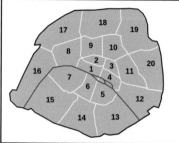

Neighborhood favorite

Pousse-Pousse
Vegan & raw restaurant

- 🛥 7 rue Notre Dame de Lorette
  cross street: rue Saint-Lazare
- 📞 01 53 16 10 81
- ⊖ Métro: Saint-Georges
- 🕐 Tu-Fr 12.00-14.45 and Sa
  12.00-18.00; Su occasionally
  open for brunch
- 🡥 www.poussepousse.eu

Over the last decade, this tiny, mostly raw vegan restaurant has cultivated a faithful following, and it's no wonder; the food is healthy, revitalizing, and lip-smacking good. Lawrence, the flame-haired proprietor, is often on hand to make guests feel at home in French and in English, and to answer questions about her creative carte. Portions aren't enormous, but the food is high quality, so you still feel sated even if the plates feel a little light.

Juices are fresh and delicious, and the homemade granola with fresh almond milk is a real treat.

Raw pizza, "nachos" and salads served with nut pâtés all make great main plates.

The formules vary from €9.90 for the tart of the day with a small side salad to €26.50 for the juice, soup, main plate and dessert combo.

Desserts are to-die-for delicious—all of them!

Juicers, sprouters, and dehydrators are also for sale, as well as other healthy-living accoutrements.

Reservations recommended. Terrace seating. Credit cards accepted.

Le Végétarien
Vegetarian fusion cafe & takeaway

- 65 rue du Faubourg Poissonnière
  Cross street: rue Bleue
- 01 42 47 15 14
- Métro: Cadet or Poissonniere
- Mon–Fri 12.00–15.30; closed Saturdays and Sundays

This no-frills lunch spot has catered to the local business crowd since 2009, and offers filling, good-value veg meals.

The hearty plat du jour (€7.50) includes a savory main (falafel, potato pancakes) plus a generous selection of ultra-fresh salads that might include any combination of tabouli, carrot, hummus, mixed greens, pasta, or in-season vegetables in a simple dressing.

Order and pay at the counter and the staff will deliver your food tout de suite. Terrace seating. Credit cards accepted.

VG
Vegetarian burger restaurant

 85 rue La Fayette
   Cross street: rue du Faubourg
   Possonière
☎ 01 44 63 87 37
⊖ Métro: Poissonnière
🕐 M 12.00–15.00, Tu–Sa 12.00–
   21.00, Su closed
🔖 www.my-vg.fr

One of the newest vegetarian spots on the scene is VG. This fast-casual restaurant serves up all kinds of interesting burgers, house-made French fries, vegan soups, and a quirky mélange of dishes that span the culinary spectrum from pad thai to Spanish-style tapas.

Lunch specials include a burger of choice (vegan or not), fries or soup or salad, and a drink for €9.50.

Vegans will be happy to know that several dessert options are available, including carrot cake! Wash it down with an espresso and you'll have enough fuel to get you through an afternoon at the Louvre.

Service is extremely friendly, professional, and efficient, and the dining area is sparkling clean and comfortable. Credit cards accepted

42 Degrés
Vegan raw food cafe

- ☛ 109 rue du Faubourg
  Poissonière
  Cross street: rue de Lafayette
- ☎ 09 73 65 77 88
- ⊖ Métro: Poissonière
- 🕐 Tu-Sa 12.00-22.30, Su-M
  closed
- ✦ www.42degres.fr
  www.facebook.com/42degres

This small chain dining spot with branches in Copenhagen just opened its first Paris location in December 2013.

The eclectic menu features pizzas, maki, soups, and burgers, plus a variety of decadent desserts.

A la carte items range from sushi made with parsnip "rice" and seasonal vegetables (€8.50) to a Portobello burger with kale "chips" (€14).

Desserts (€7-9) might include a chocolate mousse with oranges confites or cashew cheesecake.

The nightly dinner formule—which includes an entrée, plat, and dessert—will set you back €27, and a two-course lunch menu rings in at €14.

Credit cards accepted.

Le Centre Tout Naturellement
Vegan spa and café

- 83 bis, rue La Fayette
- 01 42 85 70 58
- Métro: Poissonnière
- M 11.00–20.00, Tu & Th 11.00–21.00, W 10.00–20.00, F 10.00–19.00, Sa 10.00–17.00; Su closed
- www.lecentrenaturo.com

It's hard not to fall immediately in love with this homey, friendly, peaceful spot tucked in the back of a pleasant courtyard.

First and foremost, it's a center of natural healing, with lots of therapies on offer including sauna, reflexology, and massage.

Secondly, it's a healthy lunch spot where you get soup, salad, and a main plate for just €10. The emphasis is on foods that your body can digest easily, which just happen to be 100-percent plant-based.

Dominique and Isabelle, the friendly proprietors, speak English and will happily explain the menu (there's just one option each day), as well as the

various treatments on offer.

This is the ideal destination to unwind before or after a long flight, when you're feeling rundown and want a shot of rejuvenation, or if you simply want to feel good while eating a wholesome meal. Cash only.

Chipotle
Omnivorous Mexican

- 20 Boulevard Montmartre
  Cross street: rue Drouot
- 01 45 23 12 54
- Métro:Richlieu–Drouot
- M–Su 11.00–22.00
- www.chipotle.fr

Not far from the grands magasins (department stores), this American fast-food chain often has a queue of hungry people out the door. They come for the giant burritos, burrito bowls, salads, tacos, and fajitas, all of which can be made vegan or vegetarian.

Black beans are vegan, but steer clear of the pinto beans, which are cooked with bacon.

Fresh guacamole replaces the meat in the burritos (€9), which are huge.

Tortilla chips will set you back €1 more. Try the tomatillo-red chili salsa for a spicy kick, or the roasted chili-corn salsa for something mild.

Mexican beers, soda, and other drinks available. Kid friendly. Credit cards accepted.

Bouillon Chartier
Omnivorous French

- 7 rue du Fauboug Montmartre
  Cross street: Haussmann
- (01 47 70 86 29
- ⊖ Métro: Grands Boulevards
- ● M–Su 11.30–22.00
- ✦ www.bouillon-chartier.com

The beautiful Belle Époque dining room is worth the experience alone. This fun restaurant is popular with locals and tourists alike, who come for the amazing ambience, wine, so-so food, and the general experience.

Entrees range in price from €1.80 to €6.80, and main plates are between €8.50 and €13.50. The food is sort of 1950s Julia-Child-does-French-cusine: Green beans; carrot salad; cucumber salad; endive salad, for starters. The vegetarian "special" includes a bit of everything, including spaghetti.

Desserts are copious, and the sorbets are vegan-friendly.

Kid-friendly. Credit cards accepted.

Cojean (9th)
Omnivorous healthy

- 6 rue de Seze
  Cross street: blvd de la Madeleine
- (01 40 06 08 80
- ⊖ Métro: Madeleine
- ● M–F 08.30–18.00; Sa 10.00–18.00, Su closed
- ✦ www.cojean.com

Between La Madeleine and the Opera Garnier, this outlet in the ubiquitous Cojean chain offers all the convenience (free wifi, fast service) and vegetarian options of other locations in Paris, only with longer hours.

Juices, salads, sandwiches, and soups with loads of veg options.

Free wifi. Credit cards accepted.

Le Pain Quotidien (9th)
Omnivorous Mediterranean

- Ground floor, Galleries Lafayette department store, 99 rue de Provence
  Cross street: rue Charras
- (01 42 82 34 56
- ⊖ Métro: Havre–Caumartin
- ● M–Sa 8.30–19.00, Su closed
- ✦ www.lepainquotidien.com

New branch inside the Galleries Lafayette department store. Other branches in the 2nd, 4th, and 18th.

Rose Bakery
Omnivorous English

☛ 46 rue des Martyrs
  Cross street: rue Condorcet
☎ 01 42 82 12 80
⊖ Métro: Pigalle or Saint-Georges
🕐 M-Sa 9.00-17.00; closed
  Sundays

At the foot of Montmartre, away from the tourist hordes, Rose Bakery is a quiet organic oasis with a decent selection of veg items to keep hunger at bay.

Like its two other locations (3rd, pg.74, and 12th, pg.157), organic cakes and Sunday brunch are the specialties.

Soups, salads, savory tarts, and other simple, homey dishes are available every day. Mushroom ravioli with sage (€16.50) or quinoa ravioli mighit be on the menu the day you arrive.

Credit cards accepted.

Supernature
Omnivorous healthy

☛ 2 Rue de Trévise
  Cross street: rue Richer
☎ 01 47 70 21 03
  Métro: Cadet or Grands
⊖ Boulevards
🕐 M-F 12.00-14.00, 19:00-22:30;
  Sa closed; Su 11.30-16.00

Communal table brunch spot serving homemade granola with goji berries, quinoa pancakes, hearty veggie burgers, salads, fried potatoes, and other filling fare that can be veganized if necessary.

The organic Sunday brunch rings in at €20 and includes a variety of breads and confitures, granola, optional egg dishes, bottomless cups of coffee and tea, fresh-pressed juice, and savory mains like sweet potato gratin or vegetable galette.

Muffins and fruit parfaits are among the sweet offerings.

Pleasant, light-filled space with a relaxed vibe. Kid-friendly. Credit cards accepted.

10th Arrondissement

If you've seen the wonderfully whimsical Jean-Pierre Jeunet film *Amélie*, you'll recognize Canal Saint-Martin, the tree-lined waterway where the film's protagonist liked to partake in a favorite pastime: skipping stones across the shadowy green water.

Gliding through the trendy 10th arrondissement toward the Seine, the canal is just one of many pleasures this quartier has to offer. A lively café scene, fabulous picnicking spots, vegan-shoe shopping, and top-notch Indian food can all be found here.

Probably the best arrondissement in the city for herbivores, which is especially good news for veg voyagers taking the Eurostar or Thalys trains to or from Gare du Nord.

Neighborhood favorite

Sol Semilla
Vegan healthy cafe & superfoods store

- ☛ 23 rue des Vinaigriers
  Cross street: quai de Valmy
- ☏ 01 42 01 03 44
- ⊖ Métro: Jacques Bonsargent
- ◐ T-Sa 12.00–20.00, Su 12.00–19.00
- ↘ www.sol-semilla.fr

This hybrid restaurant/boutique specializes in organic edibles from the Amazon, and everything they serve is fresh, meat-and-dairy-free, and cent percent (100 percent) delicious.

Try the special milkshake (€4.50), made with energizing South American superfoods, or feast on the hearty menu complet (€22 large/€19 small), which includes an interesting and delectable mélange of grains, cooked vegetables, and fresh crudités, plus soup and dessert.

When you've finished relishing your meal, you can browse among the superfood selection, like maca, spirulina, and açaí, and take some goodies home to amp up your morning smoothie.

Homey décor and a resident cat make this spot a welcoming respite.

Credit cards accepted.

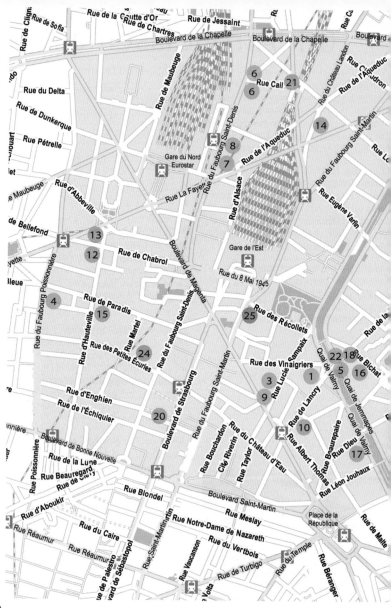

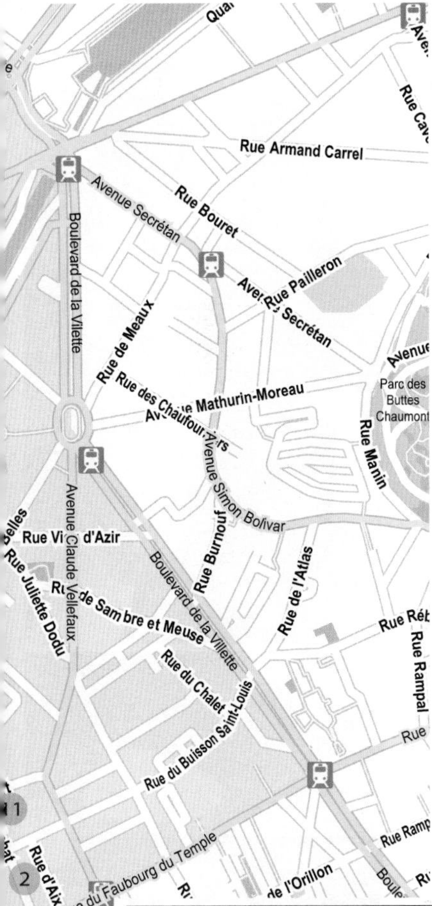

1. Sol Semilla
2. Tien Hiang
3. Bob's Juice Bar
4. Café Pinson
5. Carmen Ragosta
6. Krishna Bhavan (2 branches)
7. Saravanaa Bhavan
8. Sangeetha
9. Tuck Shop
10. El Guacamole
11. Helmut Newcake
12. Ma Kitchen
13. Mussubi
14. Massawa
15. Nanashi
16. Pink Flamingo
17. Café Sesame
18. Ten Belles
20. Passage Brady
21. Rue Cail
22. Carmen Ragosta (p.37)
23. Non-leather shoes #1 (p.37)
24. Chambres de la Grande Porte (p.13)
25. Sivananda Yoga Center (p.39, 44)

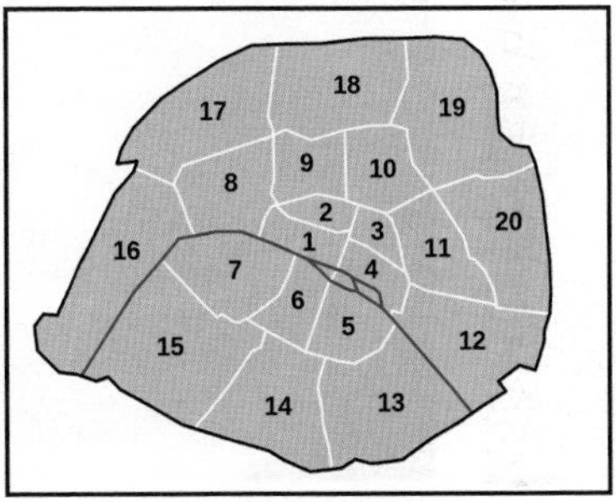

- 100% vegetarian restaurant
- restaurant/cafe
- shop
- hotel/ hostel
- cookery school/caterer
- local group/ organisation

129

Tien Hiang
Vegan Asian restaurant

☛ 14 rue Bichat
cross street: Belleville

☎ 01 42 00 08 23

⊖ Métro: Goncourt

🕙 W–M 12.00–15.00 and 18.30–
23.00 Closed Tu

🔖 www.tien-hiang.fr

If the thought of steamed dumplings, spicy noodle soups, and faux-meat stir-fries whets your appetite, reserve a table at Tien Hiang tout de suite.

The vast menu covers the most flavorful regions of Asia, from Chinese dim sum (€4–6) to Vietnamese crêpes (€7.50). The marmite selection—savory stews cooked and served in a little clay pot—are particularly delectable.

Traditional Asian desserts and a few non-dairy ice creams available for dessert.

Beer, tea, and soft drinks served.

Kid-friendly. Dog-friendly. Credit cards accepted.

Bob's Juice Bar
Vegetarian healthy cafe

- 📍 15 Rue Lucien Sampaix
  Cross street: Magenta
- ☎ 09 50 06 36 18
- ⊖ Métro: Jacques Bonsergent or République
- 🕐 M-F 7:30-15.00; Sa 08.00-16.00, Su closed. May be closed in August.

Bob's ought to be credited with bringing "accessible veg" to the 10th. Run by a former New Yorker, this healthy-elixir and light-meals café attracts musicians, models, and other pretty-people types who come for the wheatgrass juice and other juice blends, summer gazpacho (€3.50), bagels (€3-4) and vegan sweets like rice pudding and fruit crumble.

A €10.50 formule might consist of futomaki roll, soup or salad, plus fresh-baked muffin and a just-pressed juice.

Takeaway available, too, and the nearby canal is the ideal spot to enjoy your alfresco lunch.

Kid-friendly. Dog-friendly. Credit cards accepted. Also in 3rd 18th.

Café Pinson 2 (10th)
Vegetarian restaurant

- 📍 58 rue du Faubourg Poissonnière
  Cross street: rue de Paradis
- ☎ 01 45 23 59 42
- ⊖ Métro: Cadet or Poissonnière
- 🕐 M-W 08.30-19.00, Th-Sa 08.30-24.00, Su 10.00-17.00
- 🔗 www.cafepinson.fr

Trendy dining spot Café Pinson opened this second location less than a year after launching its first (in the 3rd), in a neighborhood which is quickly becoming the newest vegetarian food hub (VG, 42 Degrés, and Le Centre Tout Naturellement are all within a five-minute walk from here).

Like its Northern Marais predecessor, Café Pinson 2 boasts beautifully coiffed interiors (by celebrity designer Dorothée Meilichzon) and pretty, healthy food options. One or two items contain eggs, but otherwise, the menu is vegan.

Plats du jour might include miso soup with mushrooms and smoked tofu, or cauliflower salad with pumpkin seeds and vegan mayo.

Desserts include crumbles, compotes, and cakes (miam!) and to-go orders are welcome.

Kid-friendly. Credit cards accepted.

Carmen Ragosta
Vegetarian Italian restaurant & clothes store

- 📍 8 rue de la Grange aux Belles
  Cross street: quai des Jemmapes
- ☎ 01 42 90 00 71
- ⊖ Métro: Jacques Bonsergent
- 🕐 W–Su 12.00–19.00, plus one evening per week (changes from week to week); M–Tu closed
- k www.carmenragosta.com

The combination is genius: part clothing store, part restaurant. Independent designer and culinary whiz Carmen Ragosta is the woman behind the concept, and she and her adorable dog Pippo welcome diners and shoppers to enjoy her unique space.

Shop her one-of-a kind designs—jackets, pants, skirts, and blouses—and check out the alluring line of leather-free Melissa shoes.

Foodwise, the plat du jour (€12) and Sunday brunch (€16 served with wine or juice) are both vegan but can be made vegetarian (cheese added) upon request.

The tiramisu is a must for dessert; vegan and vegetarian versions available.

Credit cards accepted.

Krishna Bhavan (10th)
Vegetarian Indian

- 21 and 24 rue Cail
  Cross street: rue du Faubourg
  Saint-Denis
- 01 42 05 78 43
- Métro: La Chapelle
- M-Su 11.00-23.00
- www.krishna-bhavan.com

Paris's original Indian vegetarian restaurant now has two locations on rue Cail, directly across from each other.

Look for simple, tasty dosas (€5-6), idli (€3.50), and one of their best dishes, puri chole—chick-pea curry with puffed, deep fried bread (€6.50).

Most meals are served with two kinds of coconut chutney and sambar (spiced vegetable soup).

No alcohol, but plenty of juices, coffee and tea to keep thirst at bay.

Credit cards accepted. Also in the 5th, pg. 91.

Sangeetha
Vegetarian Indian

- 178 rue du Faubourg Saint
  Denis
  Cross street: rue La Fayette
- 01 40 35 00 00
- Métro: Magenta
- M-Su 10.30-22.30
- www.sangeethaparis.com
  Facebook Sangeetha Restaurant
  Végétarien

This friendly little spot right around the corner from Gare du Nord offers both North and South Indian specialties, including dosas, utthapam, and thalis, but Sangeetha's edge over the other veg Indian restaurants is chaat, otherwise known as Indian street snacks.

Bhel puri, sev puri, and other tasty treats brimming with the flavor of chilies, cilantro, and citrus are the house specialties, and most everything on the menu rings in at less than €10. Other possibilities include idly sambar, vada, and bonda.

Live classical Indian music on Friday nights makes the dining experience a bit more special. Credit cards accepted.

Saravanaa Bhavan
Vegetarian Indian

- ☛ 170 rue du Faubourg Saint-Denis
  Cross street: rue La Fayette
- ☏ 01 40 05 01 01
- ⊖ Métro: Magenta
- ◑ M–Su 10.30–23.00
- ↳ www.saravanabhavan.com

A five-minute walk out the front doors of the Gare du Nord train station (where the trains to and from London and Amsterdam come and go) sits this bustling restaurant—part of a global chain—serving authentic Indian classics.

Fluffy, perfectly cooked idli (€3.50) comes with sambar and chutney. Thalis come in North or South Indian varieties (€12.50), and include raita unless otherwise requested. Expertly prepared dosas (€5-7) and utthapam (thick, savory rice pancakes) are menu highlights.

Beer and wine by the bottle or glass, as well as the usual lassis, tea, and coffee.

Kid-friendly. Credit cards accepted.

Tuck Shop
Vegetarian café

- 13 rue Lucien Sampaix
  Cross street: Magenta
- (09 80 72 95 40
- Métro: Jacques Bonsergent
- M-F 9.30–17.00, Sa–Su 11.00–19.00
- www.facebook.com/tuckshop-paris

This cute vegetarian café run by a trio of Australians offers a simple menu, simple décor, and simple food that tastes good and appeals to vegan palates.

Try the open-faced sandwiches (€6), a warming pot of tea (€3), a comforting cup of hot chocolate (€4).

Daily baked-good specials might include muffins, cookies, or scones.

On hot days, you can expect iced coffees (€4.50) and frozen iced-tea pops (€2.50).

Non-dairy milks available for coffee drinks. Kid-friendly. Dog-friendly. Credit cards accepted.

El Guacamole
Omnivorous Mexican

- 37 rue Yves Toudic
  cross street: rue de Lancry
- (01 42 41 09 09
- Métro: Jacques Bonsergent
- M-Sa 12.00–23.00, Su 12.00–22.00
- www.elguacamole.fr

Small menu, but full of Mexican favorites that hit the spot when you're craving a bit of spice.

Burritos (€7.50) with guacamole, tacos (€3.50) with mushrooms or nopales (cactus), quesadillas (€3.50), and chips are the veg standouts.

The €2 aguas frescas (tamarind, watermelon, and other seasonal flavors) are worth every centime, but you might also like a cold Mexican beer (€5), margarita (€8), or glass of dairy-free horchata (€2).

Terrace seating. Credit cards accepted.

Helmut Newcake
Omnivorous gluten-free

- 36 rue Bichat
  Cross street: rue Alibert
- 09 82 59 00 39
- Métro: Goncourt
- W–Sa 12.00–20.00, Su 10.00–18.00; M–Tu closed
- www.helmutnewcake.com

The mavericks at Helmut Newcake were the first to bring no-gluten dining to Paris, way back in 2011. Today, this modern salon de thé offers gorgeous pastries and viennoiserie, Sunday brunch (€24) and daily lunch options that range from sandwiches to pizza.

Vegan options aplenty, including soups, salads, tarts, and banana bread.

This is also a good place to stock up on gluten-free baking mixes, pastas, and other packaged treats to make at home.

Credit cards accepted.

Ma Kitchen
Omnivorous Korean

- 85 rue d'Hauteville
  Cross street: rue de Charbol
- 09 83 07 29 96
- Métro: Poissonière
- M–F 12.00–15.30; Sa–Su closed
- www.facebook.com/makitchen1

The long line out the door hints at the popularity of this Korean cantine offering a new take on that famous dish, bi bim bap.

Look for their vegan version (€9.50) to contain unusual rice blends, a choice of six intriguing vegetable dishes, and house-made sauces with an edge (mint, sesame). Choose four ingredients for your bowl, and then prepare to feast.

Soups, sandwiches, and drinks also available to eat in, or to go.

Credit cards accepted.

Massawa
Omnivorous Ethiopian

☛ 22 rue de Chateau Landon
   Cross street: Louis Blanc

☏ 09 50 84 55 05

⊖ Métro: Chateau Landon or Louis
   Blanc

🕑 M–F 11.30– 23h30, Sa–Su
   16.00–23.30

Plenty of vegetarian appetizers here, including avocado salad (€5) and lentil salad (€4.50), but you won't really need a first course if you plan to order any of the vegetarian plates (€9-10). Not only are they the cheapest in town, but likely the most filling, too. Injera has just the right amount of tang.

Mineral water (€3), wine by the glass (€2.50) and other drinks available.

Credit cards accepted.

Mussubi
Omnivorous Japanese

☛ 89 rue d'Hauteville
   Cross street: rue de Charbol

☏ 01 42 46 31 02

⊖ Métro: Poissonière

🕑 M–F 12.00–15.00

↖ www.mussubi.fr

Right next door to the hottest Korean cantine in town sits this tiny Japanese eatery where vegetarian bento boxes, futomaki rolls, and other delicacies await.

The daily vegan bento (€12) might include brown rice, braised tofu cake, marinated vegetables, and yam with miso–basil sauce. Soups, salads, and daily sushi rolls such as edamame or shiitake mushroom.

Credit cards accepted.

Nanashi
Omnivorous Japanese

☛ 31 rue de Paradis
   Cross street: rue de Hauteville

☏ 01 40 22 05 55

⊖ Métro: Poissonière

🕑 M–Sa 12.00–00.00, Su 12.00–
   18.00

↖ www.nanashi.fr

Like its sister restaurants in the 3rd and 6th, this vegan-friendly Japanese cantine and bento bar offers three different price structures: To-go (€10), dine-in (€14), and evening / weekends (€16).

Vegetarians can choose from tasty daily offerings including tofu galette with eggplant or a salad of potatoes, fennel, red onion and zucchini.

Credit cards accepted.

Pink Flamingo
Omnivorous pizza

- 📍 67 rue Bichat
  Cross street: rue de la Grange
  aux Belles
- 📞 01 42 02 31 70
- ⊖ Métro: Jacques Bonsergent
- 🕐 Tu–Sa 12.00–15.00 and 19.00–
  23.00; Su 13.00–23.00; M
  closed
- 🔖 www.pinkflamingopizza.com

When you order one of Pink Flamingo's organic pizzas to-go, you have the option of having it delivered to your picnic spot along the canal. (They give you a pink balloon for easy spotting.)

The Aphrodite pie has hummus instead of tomato sauce and grilled eggplant (€13); the Gandhi is topped with baba ganoush and spinach (€13). Any pizza can be made vegan on request.

Beer, wine and other drinks for to-go and eat-in orders. €1 discount for takeaway.

Credit cards accepted.

Café Sesame
Omnivorous café

- 📍 51 quai de Valmy
  Cross street: rue du Faubourg
  du Temple
- 📞 01 42 49 03 21
- ⊖ Métro: République
- 🕐 M–F 9.00–24.00, Sa–Su 10.00–
  24.00
- 🔖 www.au-sesame.com

The big draw to this small but welcoming café is its location. Right on the Canal Saint-Martin, AKA hipster heaven. In summer, a couple of tables are squeezed onto the sidewalk, giving diners a chance to people-watch and enjoy the canal culture.

Lunch specials range from €10.50 to €13.50 and might include a soups-and-bagel combo or the addition of quiche or pasta.

The a la carte menu includes soups (€5), quinoa salad (€6), and pasta with seasonal vegetables (€12).

The drinks menu is vast and varied, including smoothies (€5), Italian sodas (€2), margaritas (€8), wine and coffee.

Regular themed food nights and art exhibits keep it fun and interesting.

Kid-friendly. Credit cards accepted.

Ten Belles
Omnivorous café

☛ 10 Rue de la Grange aux Belles
  Cross street: quai de Valmy

☎ 01 42 40 90 78

⊖ Métro: Colonel Fabien

🕑 M–F 8.00–18.00; S–Su 9.00–
  19.00. Closed most of August.

⚲ www.facebook.com/TenBelles

Pop into this hipster hotspot for strong and tasty filter coffee, pastries, and cakes (€3.50–4.50), and light lunch items like pasta salad with eggplant, olives, and basil (€6.50). Small and cozy with a tiny mezzanine with extra seating.

Free wifi. Credit cards accepted.

Passage Brady
Street of Indian restaurants

☛ 33 boulevard de Strasbourg to
  46 rue du Faubourg Saint-
  Denis

⊖ Métro: Chateau d'Eau

Of all of Paris's 19th century covered arcades, Passage Brady is probably the most rundown and funky; crammed full of South Indian restaurants all vying for your business. Passing through the curry-scented air can feel a bit overwhelming, but shouldn't be missed for lovers of cheap, authentic curries and filling rice plates.

Several Indian markets selling incense, Marmite, and tropical fruits make interesting pit-stops along the menu crawl.

You can also pick up spicy snack mixes to eat while watching first-run Bollywood films at the nearby Brady Cinema (39 blvd de Strasbourg).

Rue Cail
Sri Lankan restaurants and shops

⊖ Métro: La Chapelle

Known locally as "Little Jaffa" for the number of Sri Lankan restaurants and businesses clustered in this area, rue Cail, in particular, is loaded with South Asian restaurants, South Asian grocery stores, and plenty of opportunity for a spicy meal.

The food at Chettinadu Mess (15 rue Cail) gets a nod for the spiciest food in Paris; the friendliest spot in the 'hood might be newcomer Nalas Aappakadai (54 rue Louis Blanc, cross street rue Cail).

Neighboring streets rue Perdonnet and rue du Faubourg Saint-Denis are also lined with restaurants, grocery stores, sari shops, Bollywood music stores, and other South Asian markets.

EAST SIDE BURGERS
RESTAURANT VEGETARIEN
FAST-FOOD . SUR PLACE . A EMPORTER
09.67.00.78.72
FAST FOOD
VEGETARIEN
OUVERT
DU
MARDI
AU
SUR PLACE
OU A
EMPORTER
FAST FOOD
VEGETARIEN
BURGERS
HOT-DOGS
FRITES
MAISON
QUICHES
EAST SIDE BURGERS
BASIL

11th Arrondissement

The onzième is one Paris neighborhood that's undergone some serious changes in the last decade.

Home to the city's major woodworking industry throughout the Middle Ages and into the Renaissance era, those ancient ateliers (workshops) have been reclaimed and turned into artists' live-work spaces.

Once an affordable neighborhood, the 11th is officially bobo (bourgeois bohemian) ground zero, which means plenty of hipster restaurants, kid-friendly parks, upscale boulangeries, and spendy boutiques.

Some parts of the arrondissement are still a bit rough around the edges; you see this in the Oberkampf neighborhood, where bars, graffiti, and some of the city's best vegetarian food options reign.

Neighborhood favorite

East Side Burgers
Vegetarian

- ☛ 60 blvd Voltaire
  Cross street: Richard Lenoir
- ⊖ Métro: Saint-Ambroise
- 🕐 Tu-Th 12.00-18.00, F-Sa 12.00-20.00; Su-M closed. Closed most of August.
- ↖ www.eastsideburgers.fr

New York culture has invaded Paris, and nowhere is this more evident than at East Side Burgers, a "Brooklyn style" burger bar with the best meatless burgers in town.

Try the Popeye with—you guessed it—spinach (€5.95) or the Forestier, with mushrooms (€5.95). All burgers can be made with vegan cheese on request.

Vegan hot dogs (€3.60), quiches, cookies, and even vegan cheesecake available.

Frites or coleslaw are an extra €2.50, or you can get them as part of the daily lunch special, along with a drink (€9).

Downstairs dining room and a few seats on the terrace, or take your order for *emporter* (to-go). Credit cards accepted.

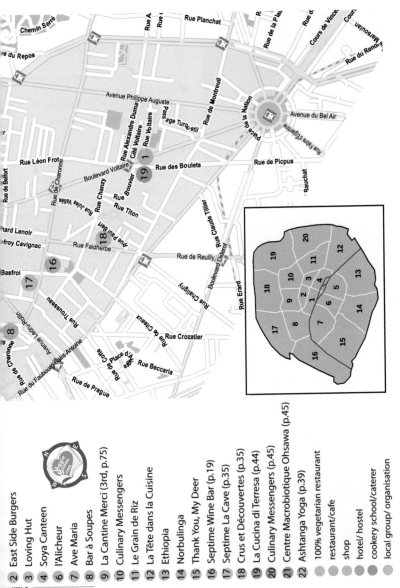

2 East Side Burgers
3 Loving Hut
4 Soya Canteen
6 l'Alicheur
7 Ave Maria
8 Bar à Soupes
9 La Cantine Merci (3rd, p.75)
10 Culinary Messengers
11 Le Grain de Riz
12 La Tête dans la Cuisine
13 Ethiopia
14 Norbulinga
15 Thank You, My Deer
16 Septime Wine Bar (p.19)
17 Septime La Cave (p.35)
18 Crus et Découvertes (p.35)
19 La Cucina di Terresa (p.44)
20 Culinary Messengers (p.45)
21 Centre Macrobiotique Ohsawa (p.45)
22 Ashtanga Yoga (p.39)

● 100% vegetarian restaurant
● restaurant/cafe
● shop
● hotel/ hostel
● cookery school/caterer
● local group/ organisation

143

© la cucina di terrESa

La Cucina di Terresa
Vegetarian restaurant at home

- 🖝 rue Voltaire/Private residence
  Cross street: blvd Voltaire
- ⊖ Métro: rue des Boulets
- 🕓 Hours vary
- 🖊 lacucinaditerresa@gmail.com
  Facebook Cucina Di Terresa

When you dine *chez Terresa*, you experience a truly unique culinary adventure. At her *table d'hôte*, you are more than just a client being served a delectable organic meal; you are her friends for the evening, and she prepares each plate with the same love and care that she would her nearest and dearest.

Each ingredient selected is exquisite— from the organic vegetables and artisan grains right down to the *fleur de sel* and freshly picked herbs and spices. You really taste the difference in Terresa's cooking, which she has perfected into an art form. Vegan and gluten-free meals always available, and diners have the choice of dining at her home or having Terresa prepare a meal for you in the kitchen of your choosing. A not-to-be missed Parisian experience.

Menus vary according to season but might include an entrée of bruschetta with chard and roast garlic; a main plate of farinata (savory chickpea cake) with seasonal vegetables and Italian olive oil; a green tomato tart with fresh herbs; and almond blanc-mange with rhubarb and citrus.

Cash only. See also pg. 34, 44, 215.

Loving Hut
Vegan Chinese & fusion fast food

- 92 blvd Beaumarchais
  Cross street: rue Saint-Claude
- 01 48 06 43 84
- Métro: Saint-Sébastian Froissart
- M-Sa 12.00-15.00 and 19.00-22.30; Su closed. Closed most of August.
- www.paris.lovinghut.fr

This amazing chain does so much for the local vegan community, including doling out generous free samples at Paris Vegan Day, VegFest Paris, and other veg festivals. They put the "Loving" in Loving Hut!

Entrées include spring rolls (€7) , samosas (€6.50) and salads (€6.50–9.50).

Main plates are tasty and filling, especially the mushroom crêpe (€14.50) with side salad, and the vermicelli noodles with fake meat, vegetables, and deep-friend eggless egg-rolls (€15).

Desserts range from banana splits to cheesecakes.

No alcohol, but tea or coffee with soymilk, near-beer, and fruit juices are available.

Small *épicerie* inside where you can buy vegan pâté and mayonnaise, Vegusto cheeses, cook books, frozen croissants and vegan *pain au chocolat*.

Credit cards accepted.

Soya Cantine
Vegetarian fusion

☛ 20 rue de la Pierre Levée
   Cross street: rue de la Fontaine
   au Roi

☏ 01 48 06 33 02

⊖ Métro: Goncourt or République

◑ F 12.00–15.30, 19.00–23.00; Sa
   11.00–23.00, Su 11.00–16.30

↘ www.soya75.fr

Vegetarians with food allergies adore this earthy, light-filled restaurant near Canal St. Martin. Big communal tables, a resident cat, and all-you-can-drink herb tea make for a home-away-from home feel, but it's the wholesome food that keeps people coming back for more.

Giant Mediterranean mezze plates (€17.50) are always vegan and always filling, as are rich stews, and wholesome grains, soups and breads.

For a stuff-your-face feast, make a reservation for the €25 Sunday brunch buffet.

Dog-friendly. Credit cards accepted.

147

l'Alicheur
Omnivorous Cambodian restaurant

- ☛ 96 rue Saint-Maur
  Cross street: Oberkampf
- ☎ 01 43 38 61 38
- ⊖ Métro: Rue Saint-Maur or Parmentier
- ◕ M–F 12.00–15.30 and 19.30–23.30; Sa–Su closed
- ⮑ www.lalicheur.com

This is healthy Cambodian food, meaning no added oil, no gluten, and plenty of fresh ingredients.

Herbivores can choose among tofu or vegetable sandwiches (€6.90), soups, salads and main plates (€6.70) composed of noodles, seasonal vegetables, and fragrant herbs like lemongrass and tamarind, and snacks such as spring rolls and sticky rice with banana.

Daily menus (€8–13.10) with entrée, plat, and dessert are a possibility, and beer and a few vegan desserts are also on the menu.

Seating is extremely limited, but to-go orders are a popular option. Credit cards accepted.

Ave Maria
Omnivorous fusion

- ☛ 1 Rue Jacquard
  Cross street: Parmentier
- ☎ 01 47 00 61 73
- ⊖ Métro: Parmentier
- ◕ M–Su 19.00–01.30
- ⮑ www.facebook.com/pages/AVE-MARIA/562613707082444

This festive little spot near the Oberkampf nightlife hub offers everyone who enters the chance to wash away worries with a tropical drink and huge portions of food inspired from the warmer spots on the planet. Vintage photos, piñatas, and colorful art hang from every spare inch inside the small dining room, which gets noisier as the evening progresses.

Main dishes range from €17–22 and include Voyage à Madras, eggplant stuffed with tomato, chickpeas, grains, caramelized onions, and Indian spices (vegans should ask for it sans fromage). The Empadao de Palmita is a huge wedge of savory pie served with a generous side salad.

Expect loud music, exotic cocktails that you can order by the pichet (small pitcher) or jumbo-sized litres, plus beer (€3–5), wine, and soft drinks.

The perfect spot to get revved up before a night out on the town. Terrace seating. Cash only.

Bar à Soupes
Omnivorous healthy

- 📍 33 rue de Charonne
  Cross street: Ledru-Rollin
- 📞 01 43 57 53 79
- 🚇 Métro: Ledru Rollin
- 🕐 M–Sa 12.00–15.00 and 18.30–22.30; Su closed.
  Closed most of August
- 🔗 www.lebarasoupes.com

If you ever wondered how Parisians stay so slim, you'll find the answer to that riddle here. It's soup, soup, and more soup—filling and nourishing, yet light on calories. Six soothing varieties are prepared each morning at this friendly spot, using vegetables and fruits that are fresh and in season. Vegetarian possibilities run the gamut from crème of carrot with coconut milk to fresh peas with mint to lentil with Indian spices to "bloody Mary" gazpacho.

The daily lunch special (€10.40) includes a bowl of soup and bread, salad or dessert, and a glass of wine, coffee, or iced tea.

If you prefer to take your soup-to-go, you can choose between small, medium, or large sizes (€3.70–5.90).

Credit cards accepted.

Culinary Messengers: Le Comptoir Japonais
Omnivorous Japanese restaurant

- 📍 3 rue Ternaux
  Cross street: Oberkampf
- 📞 06 10 24 06 53
- 🚇 Métro: Parmentier
- 🕐 M–Su 11.00–21.00
- 🔗 www.culinary-messengers.com

An intimate restaurant serving deliciously modern takes on traditional Japanese cuisine.

Vegetarian plat du jour or vegan bento (€12.50) includes rice and perfectly cooked vegetables. The soupe du jour is €5.80 for two people.

Yummy vegan tofu cheesecake (€3.50) is made by master chef Valérie, who lived in Japan for 20 years and knows her way around both sweets and healthy Japanese food. A pleasant spot in a hip part of town.

Credit cards accepted.

Le Grain de Riz
Omnivorous Vietnamese restaurant

- 49 rue Godefroy Cavaignac
  Cross street: Ledru Rollin
- (01 44 93 00 08
- ⊖ Métro: Voltaire
- ◐ M–Sa 11.30–17.00 and 17.30–
  22.30; Su closed
- ↸ www.legrainderiz.free.fr

A hole-in-the-wall Vietnamese joint with friendly service and a small but tasty veg menu. It works best if you tell the woman behind the counter that you're vegetarian, and let her serve you. It's guaranteed to taste good, as the constant coming-and-going of to-go customers can attest.

Try the bo bun (€10) or rice with tofu and vegetables; the nem au légumes are tasty, too.

Vietnamese desserts, beer, and tea available.

Cash only.

La Tête dans la Cuisine
Omnivorous healthy

- 29 rue Jean-Pierre-Timbaud
  Cross street: boulevard Richard Lenoir
- (01 43 55 04 20
- ⊖ Métro Oberkampf or Parmentier
- ◐ M–Sa 10.00–16.00, Su closed
- ↸ www.facebook.com/
  Latetedanslacuisine

Daily menus (€7-11) at this small, casual eatery allow you to choose among interesting salads, soups, quiches, and savory tarts.

The à la carte menu includes bagels (€6) and a variety of desserts, including tapioca with coconut milk.

Beer (€3) and wine (€3.50) and soft drinks available.

Kid-friendly. Credit cards accepted.

Ethiopia
Omnivorous Ethiopian

- 89 rue du Chemin Vert
  Cross street: rue Pétion
- (01 49 29 99 68
- ⊖ Métro: Voltaire or Père Lachaise
- ◐ T–Su 12.30–16.00, 19.00–
  00.30; M closed
- ↸ www.restaurant-ethiopia.com

Service is warm and welcoming and the food is tasty at this longtime neighborhood favorite.

The vegetarian platter (€38 for two) is loaded with an assortment of veggies including spiced green beans, salad, lentils, and spinach. A la carte options (€5–8.50) exist too, in case you just want a heaping helping of spiced split peas instead of the full monty.

Desserts are limited to fruit salad (€6) and non-vegan ice creams.

Washed it all down with the gingery house cocktail (€5) or tropical fruit juice (€3).

Credit cards accepted.

Norbulinga
Omnivorous Tibetan restaurant

- 118 rue Amelot
  Cross street: rue de Crussol
- 01 47 00 90 18
- Métro: Oberkampf or Filles du Calvaire
- M–Sa 12.00–14.00 and 19.00–23.00; Su closed

You'll feel at home in this welcoming Nepalese/Tibetan restaurant, with its exposed stone walls and prominent photos of the Dalai Lama on display.

A fixed price menu (€19) is one of many possibilities. À la carte momo, noodle dishes, savory crepes, and soups are other possibilities.

Beer and wine served. Credit cards accepted.

Thank You, My Deer
Omnivorous gluten-free cafe

- 112 rue Saint-Maur
  Cross street: rue Oberkampf
- 01 71 93 16 24
- Métro: Parmentier or Rue Saint-Maur
- Tu & F 10.00–18.00, W–Th 08.00–18.00, Sa–Su 12.00–18.00
- www.thankyoumydeer.com
  Facebook Thank you, my deer

Jana and Sonia, two twenty-something Slovakians who met at business school in Paris back in 2006, filled a neighborhood niche when they launched Thank You, My Deer in April 2013. Bright and cheerful, the tiny gluten-free café in the trendy Oberkampf neighborhood serves supercharged coffee, muffins (€3.50), cakes, salads (€9) and sandwiches (€7.50).

Homemade hummus, veg pâté, and super-trendy kale salad sometimes make an appearance on the menu.

Kid-friendly. Terrace seating. Dog-friendly. Credit cards accepted.

12th Arrondissement

Like many Parisian neighborhoods, the 12th is a blend of old and new architecture, and young and old populations. Butting up to the famous Bastille landmark on one end, it hugs the Seine straight to the edge of the city, where it give way to the beautiful forest known as the bois de Vincennes.

Classical theater and opera lovers come to the 12th to catch live performances at the Bastille opera house, while film aficionados flock to the Cinématheque for films and colloid-oriented art exhibitions.

Whatever your reasons are for hitting the 12th, you're never too far from a good vegetarian meal.

Neighborhood Favorite

The Gentle Gourmet Café
Vegan French

🖝 24 Boulevard de la Bastille
   Cross street: rue Jules César
📞 01 43 43 48 49
⊖ Métro: Bastille
🕘 M–Su 09.00–23.00
🔖 www.gentlegourmetcafe.com

The Franco-American Brown–Pivain family made a big splash in 2009 when it launched Paris's first-ever vegan B&B and founded the city's biggest vegan celebration, Paris Vegan Day. In 2012, the B&B closed, but the brand still expanded with the Gentle Gourmet Café, where newcomers and repeat customers alike are enticed by warm-from-the-oven croissants, meat-free burgers, and tempting sweets based on traditional French recipes.

Raw lasagna with cashew cream (€14), savory pie with mushrooms and cabbage (€17) and seitan with fig reduction sauce and garlic polenta (€22) are some of the enticing possibilities.

Expect bi-lingual service (French–English) and delicious desserts like tarte tatin (€7) and raspberry tart (€7). The only thing missing here is a license to serve alcohol, but BYOB is welcomed. Kid-friendly. Terrace seating. Dog-friendly. Credit cards accepted

153

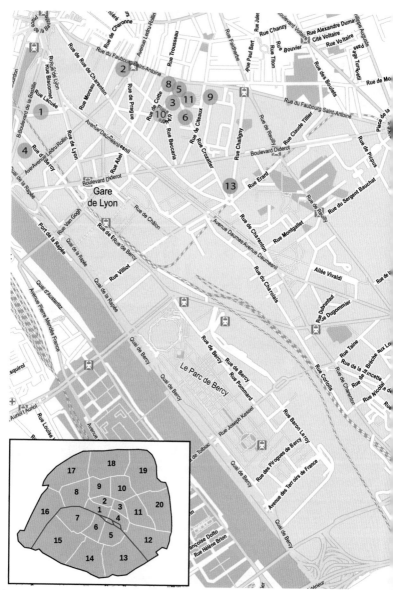

12th Arrondissement

1. Gentle Gourmet
2. HEMA
3. La Ruche à Miel
4. Rose Bakery Culture
5. Paya Thai
6. L'Adelita
7. Raimo
8. Pink Flamingo
9. Le Siffleur de Ballons (p.35)
10. Marché d'Aligre
11. Bio Génération (p.31)
12. Marché Cours de Vincennes (p.33)
13. Hotel Mistral (p.14)

- 100% vegetarian restaurant
- restaurant/cafe
- shop
- hotel/ hostel
- cookery school/caterer
- local group/ organisation

HEMA
Omnivorous store

- ☛ 86 rue du Faubourg St. Antoine
  Cross street: Ledru Rollin
- ⊖ Métro: Ledru Rollin
- 🕐 M–Sa 10.00–20.00; closed Sundays
- ↳ www.hema.fr

This Dutch Target–like chain is a new arrival on the Paris shopping scene, and one of best spots in town to stock up on convenience foods like that hard-to-procure-in-Paris favorite, peanut butter. Dried fruit-and-nut blends, chocolate-covered pretzels, potato chips, and other health-food antitheses beckon from the shelves, as do incredible cheap household items like plates, napkins, and candles. Other outlets include Gare St. Lazare, Gare du Nord, and Les Halles.

Credit cards accepted.

La Ruche à Miel
Omnivorous Algerian restaurant/tea shop

- ☛ 19 rue d'Aligre
  Cross street: rue Crozatier
- 📞 01 43 41 27 10
- ⊖ Métro: Ledru–Rollin
- 🕐 Tu–Sa 9.00–19.00, Su 9.00–18.00; M closed
- ↳ Facebook La ruche a Miel

This permanent cafe and tea shop in the heart of one of the liveliest market streets is an unexpected veg oasis. Stop in for delicious North African snacks, including m'semmen (vegan crepes stuffed with peppers and tomatoes; ask them to heat it up) and the crunchy semolina bread called kesra. Mint tea and sticky sweets (most made with honey, but ask to confirm) are other possibilities. Try the garlic-infused kesra (€1.50) for a memorable snack, or go for the vegetarian (actually vegan) couscous lunch for €10.90 (or €12 at dinner).

Terrace seats. Credit cards accepted.

Paya Thai
Omnivorous Thai

- ☛ 30 rue d'Aligre
  Cross street: rue du Faubourg Saint-Antoine
- 📞 09 50 96 10 00
- ⊖ Métro: Ledru Rollin
- 🕐 Tu–Su 12.00–14.30 and 19.00–22.30; M closed
- ↳ www.paya-thai.fr

In the thick of the Marché d'Aligre is this friendly Thai restaurant with a good selection of veg dishes, including soups and curries.

The tom kha (€10.50) tastes of lemongrass and kaffir lime leaves—in other words, really good. Old standbys pad Thai with tofu (€12.50) and pad pak (fried vegetables with tofu) are well-prepared here. Portions are on the small side, but the flavors compensate.

Sticky rice with mango and coconut milk is a must for dessert.

Beer, wine and soft drinks available,

plus coconut juice and other tropical drinks.

Credit cards accepted.

Rose Bakery Culture
Omnivorous French-English fusion

🖝 10 blvd de la Bastille (inside La Maison Rouge Fondation Antoine de Galbert)
   Cross street: rue de Bercy
☎ 01 46 28 21 14
⊖ Métro: quai de la Rapée
◐ W-Su 11.00-19.00; Th 11.00-21.00; M-Tu closed
↖ www.lamaisonrouge.org

This cute, casual spot inside the Maison Rouge contemporary art space is a dependable stop for mostly-organic sweet and savory snacks and more substantial lunch plates.

Soups, salads, risottos, and tarts are the Rose Bakery hallmarks, and that's no different here, but the difference is the access to modern art, music, and other cultural events. The decor changes every three months, as do the Maison Rouge's art exhibits, but one thing that remains constant is the quality of the food.

If you don't want to make the two-block walk up the street to the Gentle Gourmet, you might feel OK about shelling out €17 for the vegan salad plate.

Kid-friendly. Credit cards accepted.

Also in the 3rd (pg.74) and 9th (pg.126).

L'Adelita
Omnivorous Mexican

🖝 73 rue Crozatier
   Cross street: rue d'Aligre
☎ 01 46 28 79 68
⊖ Métro: Ledru Rollin or Faidherbe Chaligny
◐ Tu-Sa 12.00-15.00 and 19.00-22.00; M 12.00-15.00; Su closed
↖ www.ladelita.com

Nopales, mushrooms, rice, beans, guacamole and salsa are used in many tasty combinations at this cheap and cheerful spot. Friendly service, and nice sidewalk tables for warm days.

Veg entrées (€5) cover the usual bases: guacamole, nachos, and quesadillas, while main plates (€3-8.50) include burritos, tacos, and campechanas, which are tortillas stuffed with cactus, spinach, tomatoes, onions, and corn.

Mexican beer, margaritas (€5) and other drinks available.

Terrace seating . Credit cards accepted.

...e
...rue du Faubourg
...ne

- **☎** ...47 07
- **⊖** Mé... ...edru Rollin
- **◷** Tu-Su 12.00-15.00 and 19.00-23.00; M closed
- **↖** www.pinkflamingopizza.com

Just like its other three locations throughout Paris (in the 3rd, 10th and 18th), this Pink Flamingo branch offers organic pizzas that are easily veganized on request.

The Aphrodite pie already has hummus instead of tomato sauce, plus grilled eggplant (€13), and the Gandhi is topped with baba ganoush and spinach (€13).

Beer, wine and other drinks for to-go and eat-in orders. €1 discount for takeaway. Credit cards accepted.

Raimo
Omnivorous ice-cream parlor

- **☛** 59-61 blvd de Reuilly
  Cross Street: rue de Picpus
- **☎** 01 43 43 70 17
- **⊖** Métro: Daumesnil
- **◷** M-Su 11.00-22.00
- **↖** www.raimo.fr

Dairy-free sorbets (some are made with soymilk) hit the spot on hot summer days, and Raimo's five Paris locations make it easy to get your fix. Try the Cacao (chocolate) flavor for an off-the-charts-delicious chocolately experience, or, for something a little less conventional, try the citron-basilic (lemon-basil) or noix de coco (coconut) flavors. €3 for a single scoop, or two scoops for €5.

Credit cards accepted.

Marché d'Aligre
Street and covered market

- **☛** place d'Aligre
- **⊖** Métro: Ledru Rollin
- **◷** Tu-F 9.00-13.00 and 16.00-19.30; Sa 900-13.00 and 15.30-19.30; Su 9.00-13.30; M closed
- **↖** www.marchedaligre.free.fr

This Tuesday-though-Sunday market melds the best of two worlds: Flea-market goodies and food! The festive ambience draws crowds all year 'round, and thanks to several nearby youth hostels, the vibe is young and international. Stock up on organic tomatoes, tropical fruits, and second-hand treasures, and visit the permanent shops for staples like fresh tofu and rustic breads.

13th Arrondissement

This oft-overlooked arrondissement is a study in contrasts: on the northern end, you've got modern-industrial urban renewal, with cinemas, shopping centers, and tall buildings in steel and glass; on the southern end, you've got Paris's largest Asian community tucked amid 1970s towerblocks.

At the modern *bibliothèque* (library) Marguerite Durand, named in honor of the French feminist, you can browse an impressive collection of manuscripts, postcards, and works by celebrated women writers and artists, including Colette, Sarah Bernhardt and George Sand. At the nearby 14-screen MK2 cineplex, you can take in a movie and have a drink at the cinema's bar afterward, then dance 'til dawn at Wanderlust or catch a musical performance at the Batobar, a floating nightlife spot right on the Seine.

Nearby museums include the small but interesting Museum of Sports, where you ogle wooden bicycles, watch short films, and buy beautiful vintage-reproduction posters at reasonable prices.

Neighborhood favorite

MOB
Vegan fast food restaurant

☛ 34 Quai d'Austerlitz
Cross street: pont Charles de Gaulle
(01 42 77 51 05
⊖ Métro: Gare d'Austerlitz
● M–Su 12.00–00.00
↘ www.mob-usa.com

This Brooklyn-style burger bar moved from its original location in Paris's trendy Northern Marais district to this bright, open space at Wanderlust, the city's hottest arts and entertainment venue, which also happens to contain the city's fashion and design school.

What a difference a change of place makes! The food got an upgrade along with a design makeover, and now, it's nothing but delicious burgers (€4.00–8.50), perfectly cooked fries (€1.50–2.50), American-style hot-dogs (€8), delicious dairy-free cheesecakes (€5), and the oddly intriguing "corn soup with popcorn" (€5). Burgers are messy and tasty, and come with no-bun options for people watching their carb intake.

Credit cards accepted.

159

13th Arrondissement

1. MOB
2. Green Garden
3. Exki (13th)
4. Green Pizz (13th)
5. Nuba
6. Thien-Heng
7. Tang Frères
8. Paris Store
9. Boutique Sagane (pg.37)

- 100% vegetarian restaurant
- restaurant/cafe
- shop
- hotel/ hostel
- cookery school/caterer
- local group/ organisation

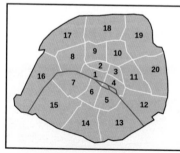

Green Garden
Vegan Asian restaurant & grocer

- ☛ 20 rue Nationale
  Cross street: blvd Massena
- ☏ 01 45 82 99 54
- ⊖ Métro: Porte d'Ivry or Olympiades
- ◑ M–Su 11.00–15.00 and 18.30–10.30

Sometimes, you just really need a steaming plate of perfectly cooked noodles with Chinese greens, which is when you want to make a detour toward Green Garden, smack in the heart of Paris's Chinatown.

Gai lan (a sort of Chinese spinach) with noodles (€8.50) is savory and nourishing, while the faux-chicken brochettes over rice hit the spot when you crave something fake-meaty. Bo bun (€7), steamed dumplings (€4), and a variety of soups keep it interesting.

No alcohol, but they offer soymilk (€2.80), juices, tea, and no-alcohol spelt beer.

The restaurant also has a little épicerie section where you can buy frozen fake meats—ham, shrimp, crab—and other vegan goodies.

Credit cards accepted.

Exki (13th)
Omnivorous healthy

- ☛ 116 Avenue de France
  Cross street: rue de Tolbiac
- ☏ 01 57 27 01 25
- ⊖ Métro: Bibliothèque François Mitterand
- ◑ M 08.00–21.30, Tu–F 08.00–22.30, Sa 12.00–21.00, Su closed
- ↘ www.exki.fr

This Belgian chain has several Paris locations, including this open, airy spot in the 13th.

Gluten-free options are labeled "SG" and vegetarian options are clearly marked "vege"; vegans will want to look out for (and steer clear of) words like *fromage* (cheese), *miel* (honey), *chèvre* (goat cheese), and *yaourt* (yogurt).

Hot mains (€3.40–7.95) include savory pies and plates full of seasoned grains or pasta with vegetables. Soups (€3.95) are almost always vegan and come with optional bread, croutons, or crackers. Salads (€1.50–5.70) are varied and flavorful, and there's also a choice of two or three vegetarian sandwiches and focaccia breads.

Desserts, wine, soft drinks, and teas available.

Lunch formule (€8.50) includes a salad, sandwich, and drink.

Terrace seating. Credit cards accepted.

Green Pizz (13th)
Omnivorous pizza

- 📍 136 blvd Vincent Auriol
  Cross street: rue Nationale
- ☎ 09 83 88 38 23
- ⊖ Métro: Nationale
- 🕐 Tu–Sa 12.00–14.30 and 19.00–22.30; Su–M closed
- 🔗 www.greenpizz.com

This pizza restaurant promises eco-friendly everything, from the organic flour and recycled to-go containers to the electric motorbikes used for deliveries.

Lunch menus from €13.90 to €19.90 include soup or salad, pizza and dessert. Several vegetarian pizzas, all of which can be veganized. Salads and soups are usually vegan.

Beer and organic bottled juices round out the drinks menu. Like this location, a sister location in the 15th also delivers hot pies to your door. Credit cards accepted

---

Nuba
Omnivorous fusion

- 📍 36 Quai d'Austerlitz
  Cross street: Pont Charles de Gaulle
- ☎ 01 76 77 34 85
- ⊖ Métro: Gare d'Austerlitz
- 🕐 Tu–Sa 12.00–15.00 and 19.00–23.00, Su 12.00–17.00, M closed
- 🔗 www.nuba-paris.fr

Part night-club, part meditation garden, part restaurant, this hip space juggles three chefs (French, Swedish and Japanese) who turn out interesting menus to please a variety of palates.

Vegan bento boxes (€15), inventive desserts like strawberry gazpacho (€7) or roasted pineapple tarte (€7) are some of the treats vegans have to look forward to.

Try to arrive before 20.00, when the crowds begin to descend. Credit cards accepted.

Thien-Heng
Omnivorous Vietnamese take-away

- 📍 50 avenue d'Ivry
  Cross Street: rue du Disque
- ☎ 01 45 82 92
- ⊖ Métro: Porte d'Ivry
- 🕐 M–Sa 08.30–19.00; Su closed

The main thing going at this tiny takeaway spot in front of Tang Frères supermarket is the banh-mi, a traditional and very tasty Vietnamese sandwich. Thien-Heng's vegan version comes with tofu, grated carrot, cucumber, cilantro (coriander), and optional jalapeno peppers.

Sandwiches (€2.30) are seasoned with the tamari-like Maggi sauce, with mayonnaise as an option; remember to say "pas de mayonnaise, s'il vous plaît" to be sure your sandwich isn't accidentally slathered with it. No possibility of eat in, but you can take your sandwich to the rooftop terrace plaza behind the restaurant and enjoy your tasty meal in the sun.

A sister shop a block away (58 rue de Choisy) serves the same sandwich, plus a few other vegan items, like samosas (€1) and seasoned rice balls. The service, however, isn't nearly as friendly at this location.

Credit cards accepted.

Tang Frères
Asian supermarket

- 📍 48 ave d'Ivry
  Cross Street: blvd Massena
- 📞 01 49 60 56 78
- 🚇 Métro: Porte d'Ivry
- 🕐 Tu-Sa 9.00-19.00; Su 9.00-13.00; M closed
- 🔗 www.facebook.com/tangofficiel

The biggest of Paris's Asian supermarkets is a treasure-trove of vegetarian delights.

Stock up on snack foods like locally prepared banana chips, Vietnamese desserts, pickled salads, and seasoned tofu.

If you're renting a short-term apartment with a kitchen, you'll want to head for the frozen food aisles, where vegetable dumplings come in myriad varieties (€3.50-5.95) and pick up a box of of tropical, dairy-free ice-cream bars in flavors like coconut, durian, and taro (€3.95).

This is also a good spot to stock up on soymilk and canned juices like

tamarind, guava, and aloe.

Outside, don't miss the fruit-juice stand (only open in the summer months), where you can buy and sip young coconuts (€2.80), fresh tropical fruit blends (€3.00), and a few non-dairy ice-cream cones (€2.80 for two scoops). The vendors are nice and happy to answer your questions.

Warning: stinky meat/fish counter at the back of the store. Credit cards accepted.

Paris Store
Asian supermarket

- 📍 44 ave d'Ivry
  Cross Street: blvd Massena
- 📞 01 44 06 88 18
- 🚇 Métro: Porte d'Ivry
- 🕐 T-Th 9.00-19.00, F-Sa 9.00-20.00, Su 9.00-13.00; M closed
- 🔗 www.paris-store.com

Tucked into the ground floor of the funky Olimpiades shopping complex, Paris Store is a smaller version of Tang Frères, with an equally veg-friendly inventory.

Young coconuts (€1.95), plain and seasoned tofu, Vietnamese desserts, fresh Asian produce and tropical fruits, and lots of snack items available throughout the store.

On the sidewalk in front of the store, pop-up vendors sell everything from fresh herbs and homemade sweets to tourists' trinkets and mobile phone cases.

Credit cards accepted.

14th Arrondissement

If you've made the trek to the 14th, you're probably headed toward something with Montparnasse in its title: Montparnasse train station, Montparnasse cemetery, or perhaps Montparnasse tower, for its 360-degree views over the Île-de-France landscape.

Also worth a visit are the Catacombs, full of the old bones of Paris's long-dead, and the small, moving Musée Jean Moulin, dedicated to the liberation of Paris and the end of WWII.

When you've had enough of the sights and are ready to tuck into something tasty, give one of these reliable spots a try.

Aquarius
Vegetarian fusion restaurant

- 40 rue de Gergovie
  Cross street: rue Decrès
- 01 45 41 36 88
- Métro: Pernety
- M–Sa 12.00–14.15 and 19.00–23.00; Su closed

A pleasant, homey interior and a vegetarian menu to match? Indeed. Vegan choices are limited to two or so rotating plates influenced by Asian cuisines, but dairy-doers will be happy with the selection of options that take inspiration from the Mediterranean, the Americas, and other corners of the globe.

Lasagna, "meat" loaf, mushroom pie, and vegan pâté are some of the possibilities. Mid-day formule (€13) includes an entrée and main plate, or main plate and dessert. On the lighter end of the spectrum, there's seaweed salad with smoked tofu (€8), and on the opposite end, there's a mixed-grill plate (€19) loaded with fake meats—grain sausage, tofu sausage, seitan steak—and gravy.

Cheesecakes, fruit tarts, and chocolatey gâteau round out the dessert menu.

Credit cards accepted.

14th Arrondissement

1. Aquarius
2. Chocolatitudes
3. Diététic Shop
4. Paradis de Fruit
5. Exki (14th)
6. Cave des Papilles (p.35)
7. Formule 1 hotel (p.13)
8. Chocolatitudes (p.46)

- 100% vegetarian restaurant
- restaurant/cafe
- shop
- hotel/ hostel
- cookery school/caterer
- local group/ organisation

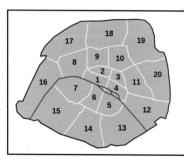

ChocoLatitudes
Vegetarian chocolate shop

- 57 Rue Daguerre
  Cross street: rue Gassendi
- (01 42 18 49 02
- Métro: Gaité or Raspail
- W & F 12.00-19.00, Th 12.00-20.00, Sa 11.00-19.00, Su 11.00-14.00 and 16.00-19.00, M-Tu closed. Closed most of August.
- www.chocolatitudes.com

There's so much to love about this tiny chocolate boutique near Montparnasse cemetery.

First, there's the thick cups of hot chocolate. WITH VEGAN CHANTILLY! (That's whipped cream, for the Yanks.) Rich, decadent, and delicious, and worth a trip for this liquid experience alone.

Look for vegan Booja Booja chocolates, dairy-free spreads, raw and organic chocolates, and an endless array of gift ideas for your friends and family back home.

You'll also find chocolate-tasting classes here (see pg. 46), and monthly tarot-and-hot cocoa meetups.

Laurence, the lovely proprietor, speaks English, so don't be shy about asking questions.

Credit cards accepted.

Diététic Shop
Vegetarian & fish organic macrobiotic restaurant & health food shop

- 11 Rue Delambre
  Cross street: blvd de Montparnasse
- (01 43 35 39 79
- ⊖ Métro: Vavin
- ● M–F 12.00–15.00 and 17.00–22.30; Sa 12.00–15.00; Su closed
- ⓚ www.dieteticshop.fr/en

This is one of Paris's oldest macrobiotic restaurants, and in some ways, it still feels trapped in a '70s time warp, though in the best possible way. Communal wooden tables, hearty plates of faux meats, grains, and salads hit the spot, and reasonable prices are what to expect. Fish served, but the restaurant is mostly veg with plentiful vegan options.

Seitan and vegetables, cassoulet, and vegetable gratin (€10–12.50) are a few of the mains. Lighter plates include vegetable terrine, which comes with a gorgeous salad and bread.

You'll also find muesli, fruit compotes, and other old-school sweets on the menu.

Unlike many macro restaurants in Paris, you'll find wine on the menu here, as well as soy milk, fresh-pressed fruit and vegetable juices, tea, and coffee.

At the health food store attached to the restaurant you can pick up rice cakes, juices, and other snacks.

Credit cards accepted.

Paradis du Fruit
French healthy restaurant

- 21 blvd Edgar Quinet
  Cross street: rue de Montparnasse
- (01 40 47 53 44
- ⊖ Métro: Edgar Quinet
- ● M-Th 12.00–01.00, F-Sa 12.00–02.00, Su 12.00–01.00
- ⓚ www.leparadisdufruit.fr

This late-night chain restaurant offers "healthy" food in uniformly bright and cheerful dining rooms throughout the city.

The vegetarian options range from gazpacho (€7.90) and toasted sandwiches (€6.90) to tofu coconut curry (€12.90) and DIY composed plates (€12.50–16.50) that might include rice, green salad, steamed vegetables, French fries, guacamole, or toasted pita. All veg items are marked with a little green angel. Vegan options available on request.

To drink, look for juice drinks (€7), mojitos, piña coladas, and cosmopolitans (€10.90), bottled water, and wine by the glass or bottle.

Terrace seating. Credit cards accepted.

Exki (14th)
Omnivorous healthy

☛ 82 blvd du Montparnasse
Cross street: rue de
Montparnasse

☎ 01 42 18 13 27

⊖ Métro: Montparnasse Bienvenue
or Vavin

🕐 M-Th 09.00–22.00, F 08.00–
23.00, Sa 09.00–23.00, Su
09.00–22.00

🖐 www.exki.fr

Like the other outlets scattered across
Paris, this one, right in the shadow of
Montparnasse tower, offers plenty of
veg(an) and gluten-free options.

Soups (€3.95) are almost always vegan
and come with optional bread,
croutons, or crackers. Hot mains
(€3.40-7.95) include savory pies and
plates full of seasoned grains or pasta
with vegetables. Salads (€1.50-5.70)
are varied and flavorful, and there's
also a choice of two or three vegetarian sandwiches and focaccia
breads. Lunch formule (€8.50)
includes a salad, sandwich, and drink.

Desserts, wine, soft drinks, and teas
available

Relaxed and comfortable ambience,
and cleaner-than-average bathrooms.
Credit cards accepted.

15th Arrondissement

Like the neighboring 16th arrondissement, the 15th feels less commercial and more residential than many other Parisian neighborhoods. If you've found yourself here, you've probably come to see the sculptures at the Bourdelle museum, to wander the manicured lawns at Parc Citroën, or to take one of the popular Fat Tire Bicycle Tours.

Though the veg dining possibilities are more limited here, you definitely won't go hungry—just make a beeline for one of these spots, or take a pleasant stroll to the neighboring 7th for more options.

Green Pizz (15th)
Omnivorous organic pizzeria

- 🠖 32 rue de Dantzig
  Cross street: rue des Morillons
- 📞 09 66 94 37 48
- ⊖ Métro: Porte de Versailles
- 🕑 Tu–Sa 12.00–14.30 and 19.00–22.30; Su–M closed. Also open Sundays in summer.
- 🔖 www.greenpizz.com
  www.facebook.com/GreenPizz

This two-location pizza spot promises eco-friendly everything, from the organic flour and recycled to-go containers to the electric motorbikes used for deliveries.

Lunch menus from €13.90 to €19.90 include soup or salad, pizza and dessert. Look for several vegetarian pizzas (€11.50-15), all of which can be veganized. Salads (€4.80-€5) are veg-friendly, and soups (€4.80) are usually vegan.

Beer, wine, soda, and organic bottled juices round out the drinks menu.

Like this location, a sister location in the 13th also delivers hot pies to your door. Credit cards accepted.

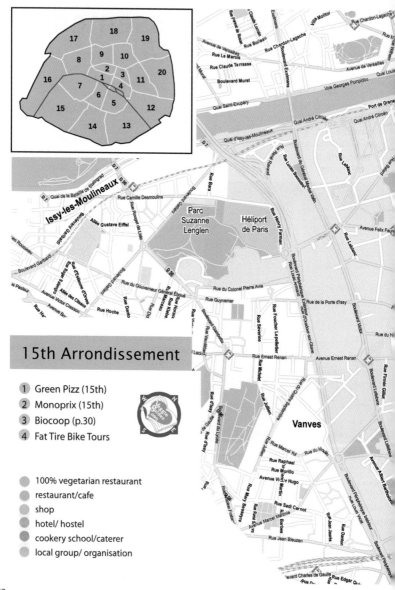

15th Arrondissement

1. Green Pizz (15th)
2. Monoprix (15th)
3. Biocoop (p.30)
4. Fat Tire Bike Tours

- 100% vegetarian restaurant
- restaurant/cafe
- shop
- hotel/ hostel
- cookery school/caterer
- local group/ organisation

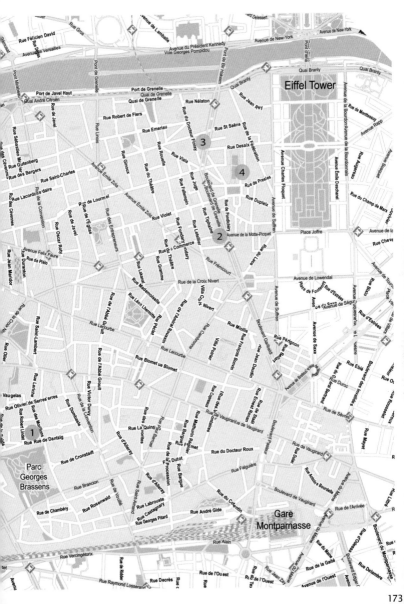

Monoprix (15th)
Omnivorous supermarket

- 2 rue de Commerce
  Cross street: ave de La Motte–Piquet
- 01 45 79 94 86
- Métro: La Motte–Piquet
- M–Sa 09.00–22.00, Su closed

When all else fails, there's always Monoprix. Perched on the corner of busy shopping street rue de Commerce, the giant superstore chain has an upstairs supermarket where scads of prefab salads and sandwiches await. In the refrigerator section you'll also find seasoned tofu, vegan burgers that can be eaten heated or straight out of the package, and an in-store *boulangerie* where you can pick up warm bread, tarts, and other sweets, and all kinds of spreads for your baguettes. Drinks, chocolate, and wine are a few more of the meat- and dairy-free things you'll discover here. Credit cards accepted.

Fat Tire Bike Tours
Bicycle tours

- Fat Tire Bike Tours, 24 rue Edgar Faure
  Cross street: Allée Marguerite Yourcenar
- 01 56 58 10 54
  In USA 866 614 6218 toll free
- Métro Edgar Faure
- www.paris.fattirebiketours.com

For visitors to the City of Light who aren't intimidated by cobblestones and the occasional unexpected thunder shower, Fat Tire Bike and City Segway Tours offer several excellent possibilities for getting well acquainted with Paris.

Friendly English-speaking guides take small groups out on cushy cruisers or two-wheel Segways and give a crash-course in local history, from the famous Tower to Napoleon's Tomb and beyond.

Hint for oenophiles: Wine is a vital component of the night-tour itinerary!

16th Arrondissement

This is the most exclusive district in Paris; a combination of upscale residential housing, chi-chi boutiques, and foreign embassies.

For such a sleepy arrondissement, there are a surprising number of museums, including the Palais de Tokyo, Musée Galliera, Musée Guimet, and Musée Marmottan-Monet.

The 16th is also the gateway to the verdant Bois de Boulogne, Paris's version of Central Park, where you can rent boats and glide across a man-made lake, have a picnic, and enjoy a stroll through the forest.

Jour
Omnivorous healthy salad bar

- 40 avenue Kléber
  Cross street: rue de Belloy
- 01 83 64 95 16
- Métro: Kleber
- M–Sa 11.45–16.30, Su closed
- www.jour.fr

Not far from the Arc de Triomphe in Paris's most upscale arrondissement sits Jour, one of the best salad bars in the city.

Select a salad base of greens—spinach, arugula (rocket), romaine—pasta, or grains (€2.80-4.80), then go to town choosing your toppings to make the custom salad of your lunchtime dreams. Artichokes, tofu, green beans, melon, corn, croutons, and other yummy choices abound (€.25-2.10).

Lunch specials start at €7.90 for a plat, dessert and drink. Soups, wraps, and savory tarts are among the other veg options. Bread (€.50), chips and a variety of vegan salad dressings to choose from.

Juice, tea, and wine too. Terrace seating. Credit Cards accepted.

Bon
Omnivorous Asian fusion

- 25 rue de La Pompe
  Cross street: rue de Passy
- 01 40 72 70 00
- Métro : La Muette
- M–Su 12.00–14.30 and 19.30–23.00w
- www.restaurantbon.fr

Upscale décor, themed rooms, and a cozy patio conspire to create a certain ambience that makes eating here a true "experience." While the Asian-inspired menu doesn't exactly overflow with vegetarian options, Bon does offer a generous handful of plates that are expertly prepared and tasty.

Spicy tomato gazpacho (€14), warm leek vinaigrette ponzu (€12), lacquered eggplant with miso sauce (€17), vegetable spring rolls (€12), and noodles with vegetables (€15) are the veg menu highlights.

To drink, look for a good wine list tea, soft drinks and fruit juices.

Free wifi. Credit cards accepted.

Tokyo Eat at the Palais de Tokyo
Omnivorous fusion restaurant

- 13 Avenue Président Wilson
  Cross street: ave d'Iéna
- 01 47 20 00 29
- Métro: Iéna
- M–Su 12.00–02.00
- www.palaisdetokyo.com/

One of the highlights of this contemporary art museum is the attached restaurant. Open, airy, and bustling at peak meal times enhanced by a live DJ spinning records, the Tokyo Eat gives good service, tasty food, and a really nice selection of veg options.

Fresh carrot–ginger juice (€5), fruit smoothies (€6) and Japanese green teas are the stars of the drinks menu. For solid sustenance, there's black rice risotto (€20), mushroom rigatoni (€14), chestnut soup with spiced-bread croutons (€8), and several expertly prepared seasonal vegetable dishes, including beet tartare (€11).

The museum gift shop makes a great post-dining stop.

Kid friendly. Terrace seating. Credit cards accepted.

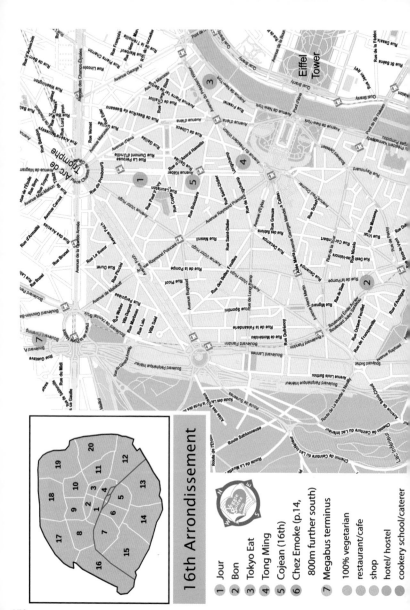

16th Arrondissement

1. Jour
2. Bon
3. Tokyo Eat
4. Tong Ming
5. Cojean (16th)
6. Chez Emoke (p.14, 800m further south)
7. Megabus terminus

- 100% vegetarian
- restaurant/cafe
- shop
- hotel/ hostel
- cookery school/caterer

Tong Ming
Omnivorous Thai restaurant

🐷 11 rue de Magdebourg
  Cross street: ave Kléber

📞 01 45 53 02 77

⊖ Métro : Trocadero or Iéna

🕐 M–F 12.00–14.30 and 19.00–23.30, Sa 19.00–23.30, Su closed

🔗 www.tongmingthai.com

Lots of veg possibilities abound at this long-established Thai restaurant near Trocadero with its amazing Eiffel Tower views.

All of the soups (€9.90) have a vegetarian version (the broth is made with mushrooms, coconut milk, and galangal), and the same goes for the curries, which can be made with or without tofu. Noodle dishes like pad Thai with tofu (€16.90) are filling and sizeable enough to be shared (though you may not want to). Lots of tofu dishes, like tofu with ginger, three-spice tofu, and garlic-ginger tofu, to be eaten with perfumed jasmine rice or sticky rice.

Friendly, helpful staff and full bar. Credit cards accepted.

Cojean (16th)
Omnivorous healthy

🐷 78 Avenue Kléber
  Cross street: rue Boissière

📞 01 47 04 73 80

⊖ Métro: Boissière

🕐 M–F 8.30–16.00, Sa–Su closed

🔗 www.cojean.fr

Like most of the other Cojeans in Paris, here you'll find toasted vegetable sandwiches (€4.90), lasagna (€8.90), vegan soups (€4.50–4.90), and salads galore (€2.90–5.90).

Look for organic juices, bubble tea, and dairy-free tapioca desserts (€2.90).

Cojean caters to the lunchtime office crowd, and both hours and ambience reflect that. Still a good spot for a light snack and something to drink.

Free wifi. Credit cards accepted.

17th Arrondissement

The 17th arrondissement might very well be Paris's most underrated in terms of tourism. On one hand, it's understandable: Besides sharing a little slice of Arc de Triomphe glory (the southwest border of the 17th nuzzles right up to it) and a celebrated park (Monceau), the 17th doesn't really possess the sexy cachet that the other districts have; but what it lacks in sexy caché it makes up for in Parisian authenticity. With a broad socio-economic spectrum you get a mixed community from every ethnic and religious background, and all the amenities that appeal to an eclectic community.

To get a good sense of what living in Paris is all about, park yourself at one of the cute hotels that dot the Batignolles neighborhood, then make the neighborhood your own while you're here. Take your tea (or coffee) at the nearest brasserie/café in the morning, stroll through a perfectly coiffed 19th-century park, visit the local bibliothèque (library), take in a movie at an art-house cinema, poke your nose into quaint and quirky secondhand shops, sip a petite cup of wheatgrass juice from a stand at the organic Saturday farmers' market, and take your evening meal at a pizzeria where fromage-free pies won't garner any funny looks from your Italian waiter.

Joy in Food
Healthy vegetarian restaurant

- ☛ 2 rue Truffaut
  Cross street: rue des Dames
- ☎ 01 43 87 96 79
- ⊖ Métro: Rome or Place Clichy
- ◕ M–F 12.00–14.30, Sa–Su closed. Closed most of August

This family-run restaurant is only open for lunch on weekdays, and draws a faithful clientele who come for the homey, hearty, and generous cooked grain-and-vegetable plates, friendly service, and cozy atmosphere. The 90 percent vegan menu includes a generous selection of dairy-free desserts.

Entrées range in price between €5 for a salad to €7 for the vegan pâté or vegetable tarte. Plat du jour (€10) is filling, but try to save room for the apple crumble (€6).

The formule (€13) includes an entrée and plat, or plat and dessert—or if you're really hungry, the €17 formule offers three courses.

Fruit juices (€3) and coffee (€2). Cash only.

17th Arrondissement

1. My Kitch'n 1
2. Joy in Food
3. My Kitch'n 2
4. Bio Prestige cafe/shop
5. Edgar Traiteur
6. Kloog Café
7. Menelik
8. Le Mont Liban
9. Onigiriya
10. Planet Thai
11. La Table Verte
12. L'Epicerie Verte
13. Marché Bio Batignolles (p.33,186)
14. Marché Couvert Batignolles (p.33)
15. Naturalia, 21 bd des Batignolles
16. Non-leather shoes #2 (p.37)
17. Megabus terminus

- 100% vegetarian restaurant
- restaurant/cafe
- shop
- hotel/ hostel
- cookery school/caterer
- local group/ organisation

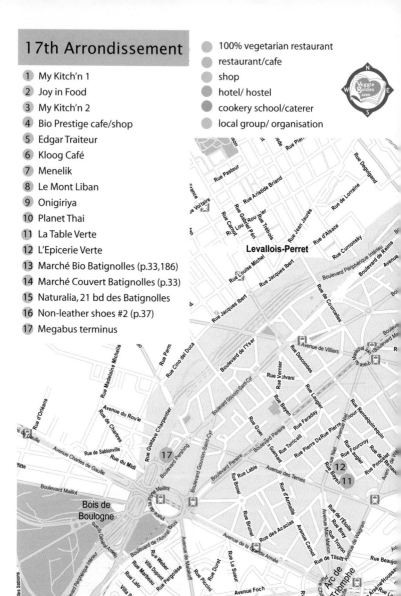

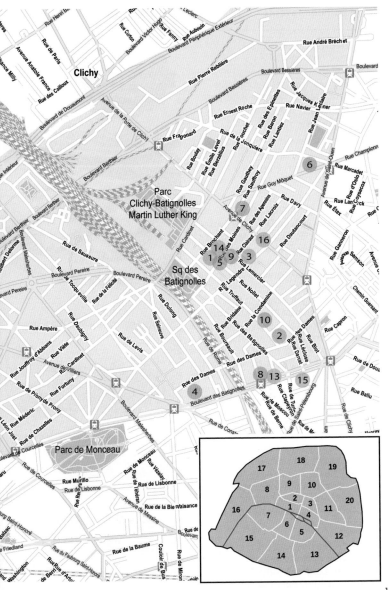

My Kitch'n
Vegan and raw food cafe

☞ Inside Marché des Batignolles indoor market, 24 rue Brochant
  Cross street: rue Lemercier

☎ 06 16 15 44 74

⊖ Métro: Brochant

◕ Tu-F 9.00-13.00 and 15.30-20.00, Sa 9.00-20.00, Su 9.00-14.00; M closed

↖ www.mykitchn.fr
  www.facebook.com/mykitchn.fr

Many Paris restaurants promise healthy, delicious food, but My Kitch'n really delivers. The homemade gluten- and soy-free burgers (€12.50) come with roasted potatoes and green garnish, and are one of the main reasons to make a detour to this fast-casual spot inside the Batignolles indoor market; the super-friendly service is another. Jennifer, the lovely English-speaking proprietor, is a fountain of knowledge and will happily explain her culinary philosophy, and share facts related to plant-based diets.

The daily soup (€4.50) might be carrot-ginger, and odds are good there'll be raw carrot cake (€4.50) or maybe a tasty fig cake with lavender icing (€3.20). Amazingly delicious green smoothies (€4.50), potent and tasty Fairtrade Marley coffee (€2.50), and imaginative sweet and savory dishes.

A small seating area inside, and take-away options galore. Children welcome. Dog-friendly. Cash only. Second location opening Sept 2014.

Batignolles Organic Market
Organic street market

- 34 boulevard des Batignolles
  (between rue des Batignolles
  and rue Boursault)
- Métro: Rome or Place de Clichy
- Saturdays 9.00–15.00

Small but sweet Saturday morning market with an interesting combination of food, household items, beauty products, and healthy foods that are all certified organic.

Look for vegan croissants, superfoods from Sol Semilla (see 10th), kale and wheatgrass shots from Madame Mustard, and booths selling skin creams scented with aromatic essential oils.

If you didn't see what you're looking for, odds are good you'll find it across the street at Naturalia.

Note: This is the Saturday Marché Biologique (organic) des Batignolles, on the south-east corner of the 17th. A few blocks away north-west along rue Lemercier is the indoor Marché Couvert (covered) des Batignolles (p.33), which houses My Kitch'n and is open the same times.

Bio Prestige
Omnivorous organic health food store and cafe

- 92 boulevard Batignolles
  Cross street: Rome
- 01 45 22 53 52
- Métro: Villiers
- M–Sa 09.00–22.00; Su closed
- www.bio-prestige-paris.fr

You'll find more than just organic beauty products, vitamins, and pantry staples at this upscale (aka expensive) natural foods store.

Inside, you'll discover an organic Italian traiteur, where you can load up on picnic foods including olives, marinated artichokes and grilled eggplant, pasta- and grain-based salads, and stuffed grape leaves. Eat inside at one of the few small tables, or take your goodies to go.

Credit cards accepted.

Edgar Traiteur
Omivorous Lebanese cafe/takeaway

- Inside Marché des Batignolles indoor market, 96bis rue Lemercier
  Cross street: 24 rue Brochant
- (06 01 06 06 06
- ⊖ Métro: Brochant
- ◑ Tu-F 09.00-13.00 and 15.30-20.00, Sa 9.00-20.00, Su 9.00-14.00; M closed
- ✦ Facebook Edgar Traiteur

With a few exceptions, nearly everything showcased inside the gleaming glass deli case is vegan.

Stuffed grape leaves (€1.20 for three), a dozen varieties of savory dips—artichoke, fig, garlic (€2.50 for 100 grams)—plus hummus and baba ganoush. The list of treats goes on and on and on, and Edgar, the amiable proprietor, will happily offer you samples. The olive selection is astounding, with 19 delicious varieties.

Tasty and affordable falafel sandwiches (€3.50), and the super-addictive little pastries stuffed with spinach and onion called fatayer (€1) are vegan and satisfying.

Eat in on the mezzanine or take your falafel to go and enjoy it at the modern Parc Martin Luther King or old-school Square Batignolles.

Credit cards accepted.

Kloog Café
Omnivorous healthy bistro

- 63 rue Guy Moquet
  Cross street: ave Saint-Ouen
- ⊖ Métro: Guy Môquet
- (01 42 29 59 18
- ◑ M-W 11.00-13.30, W-Sa 18.30-21.00; Su 10.00-14.30 and 18.30-21.00

Its distinct pink façade makes this little organic restaurant easy to spot. Step into the teeny-tiny dining room with the bright green walls and you'll discover an interesting variety of veg plates.

Run by a Franco-Norwegian couple, Kloog's menu offers a similarly eclectic blend of flavors: eggplant sushi, Thai-style coconut milk soup, French-style tartines, and carrot cake might feature on the daily menu.

Evening formule (€25) includes an entrée, plat, and dessert. À la carte menu available. Kid-friendly. Terrace seating. Credit cards accepted.

Menelik
Omnivorous Ethiopian restaurant

- 4 rue Sauffroy
  Cross street: rue de Clichy
- 01 46 27 00 82
- Métro: Brochant
- M–Su 12.00–15.00 and 19.00–23.00
- www.menelikrestaurant.com

The best Ethiopian food in Paris can be found here, at this family-run restaurant where you always get a warm welcome.

A complimentary kir (white wine and cassis syrup) comes with the menu, which you won't need, because there's only one thing to order here: The vegetarian combo plate (€12.50).

Expect a giant, dairy- and egg-free platter full of spiced lentils, split peas, perfectly-cooked spinach, potato-and-green-bean mélange, salad, and mustard-spiced lentils.

Wine, coffee, Ethiopian beer, and a variety of non-vegan desserts served.

Try to come for the Friday and Saturday night coffee ceremony. Beginning at 22.45, the dining room fills with the smell of roasting coffee beans, and a pan is passed around so you can take a good whiff, along with a nibble of traditional spiced bread. A real dining experience.

Terrace seating. English spoken. Credit cards accepted.

Le Mont Liban
Omivorous Lebanese

- 42 blvd des Batignolles
  Cross street: rue des Batignolles
- 01 45 22 35 01
- Métro: Rome or Place de Clichy
- M–Su 12.00–15.00, 19.00–23.00
- www.mont-liban.fr

Popular spot across from the Batignolles street market serves tasty Lebanese mezze plates and other dishes à la carte.

Moussaka (€6.50) pairs eggplant with chickpeas, onion, and a savory tomato sauce. The fatouche salad (€6) is seasoned sumac and features plenty of grilled pita. Moujadra (€5.50) is a filling mélange of lentils, rice, and slow-cooked onions, and if you're feeling daring, you might try the tasty fava beans cooked in garlic, tomato, and olive oil (€6.50).

When all else fails, there's always falafel (€7). Falafel sandwiches are sold next door at their other casual-dining location.

Mint tea, Lebanese beer and wines are also on the menu.

Terrace seating. Credit cards accepted.

Onigiriya
Omivorous Japanese cafe

- ☛ Marché des Batignolles indoor market, 24 rue Brochant
  Cross street: rue Lemercier
- ☎ 01 58 60 08 02
- ⊖ Métro: Brochant
- 🕔 Tu–F 09.00–13.00 and 15.30–20.00, Sa 9.00–20.00, Su 9.00–14.00; M closed

This Japanese cantine inside the covered market offers a nice selection of vegetarian options, including onigiri stuffed with miso or seaweed and vegetables (€1.50 each). Tempura vegetables (€3.00) might include sweet potato, onion, carrot, though the batter contains eggs.

For dessert, the homemade red bean cake with macha is a popular choice.

Friendly service and authentic Japanese flavor are the key components of this sweet little spot. Cash only.

Planet Thaï
Omnivorous Thai restaurant

- ☛ 28 rue Truffaut
  Cross street: rue des Dames
- ☎ 01 45 22 45 12
- ⊖ Métro Rome or Place de Clichy
- 🕔 M–Sa 12.00–15.00 and 18.00–23.00, Su 18.00–23.00
- ↖ www.planetethai.com

A Frenchman, his Thai wife, and their daughter run this tiny, authentic, and deliciously veg-friendly little eatery behind the Mairie (town hall) in the Batignolles district.

Ask for the carte végétarienne (vegetarian menu), and select among such tasty dishes as seven-vegetable spring rolls (€6 for 3), eggplant in green-curry sauce (€12), mushroom soup with coconut milk and lemongrass (€8) and black mushroom ginger noodles (€12).

Beer and wine served. Service can be slow and portions are on the small side, but the food itself is high-quality and tasty. They deliver too! Ask for "livraison" (delivery), or try the eat-in daily menu for €12 (€8.50 for take-away).

Credit cards accepted.

La Table Verte
Omnivorous healthy restaurant & shop

- 🖝 5 & 9 Rue Saussier-Leroy
  Cross street: rue Poncelet
- ☎ 01 47 64 19 68 restaurant
  01 83 96 50 77 shop
- ⊖ Métro: Ternes
- 🕐 Restaurant M–F 10.00–18.00, Sa
  10.00–17.00, Su closed.
  Shop M–F 10.00–20.00, Sa
  10.00–19.30, Su closed.
- ➘ www.lepicerieverte.com

Just off the charming shopping street Poncelet sits this hidden gem, where a filling and delicious lunch can be eaten in or taken to go. The restaurant is 90 percent vegetarian. Expect savory tarts, gratins, and salads made with organic seasonal vegetables, with plenty of vegan options.

Brunch (€20) consists of coffee or tea, fresh-pressed juice, tarte or gratin du jour with two salads, pancakes or muffin, and optional yogurt with goji berries.

Next door sits l'Epicere Verte, a well-stocked natural foods store with skin-care products, fresh breads, household goods, and more.

Terrace seating. Credit cards accepted.

My Kitch'n 2
Vegan and raw food cafe

- 🖝 82 rue Lemercier
  Cross street: rue Clairaut
- ☎ 06 16 15 44 74
- ⊖ Métro: Brochant
- 🕐 Open longer hours including evenings
- ➘ www.mykitchn.fr
  www.facebook.com/mykitchn.fr

STOP PRESS: As we go to print, a second branch of my Kitch'n is getting ready to open in September 2014 very close to the original (pg.184).

18th Arrondissement

Montmartre is one of Paris's most exciting neighborhoods. The "little village" ambience makes it ideal for strolling, from the foot of the fabled hill with its boutiques, cafés, and bars, straight up to the snow-white Sacré-Coeur basilica and its stupendous views over Paris.

A number of private museums—the Dali Museum, Musée d'Erotisme—as well as the charming Musée de Montmartre and its lovely gardens are perennial draws.

Events that take place here throughout the year, including October's Fête des Vendanges de Montmartre (Montmartre Wine Festival) and June's Fete de la Musique, bring out the crowds and add to the already-festive ambience.

Come spend the day exploring the cobbled streets and experiencing the Disney-esque vibe of Place du Tertre. At nightfall, take a seat on the steps of Sacré-Coeur and watch the street theater—jugglers, dancers, musicians—unfold before your eyes.

Toutofu: Atelier de Soja
Vegetarian Chinese café

- 25 rue Ordener
  Cross street: rue Ernestine
- Métro: Marcadet-Poissoniers
- M–Tu 17.00-19.00; F-Su 11.00-19.00, W-Th closed

This tiny, family-run restaurant specializes in house-made tofu dishes cooked in traditional Chinese styles.

Menu items include mapo tofu in a spicy sauce (€7.80) served with rice and vegetables, or stir-fried tofu with vegetables (€7.80), but you might try the French influenced green lentil salad with smoked tofu (€4.20).

Fresh soy milk, intriguing soups, and vegan desserts are other possibilities.

A takeaway counter lets you pick up prepared salads and tofu to-go. Cash only.

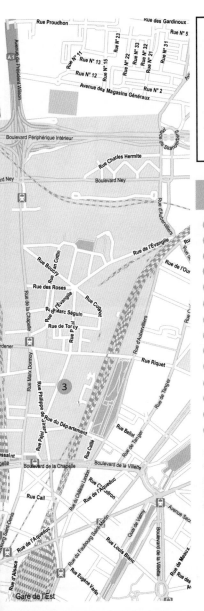

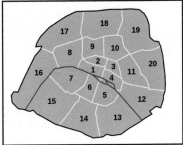

18th Arrondissement

1. Au Grain de Folie
2. Toutofu: Atelier de Soja
3. Bob's Bake Shop
4. Le Cambodge
5. Gang Seng
6. Hope Café
7. Moulin Rouge
8. Le Pain Quotidien (18th)
9. Soul Kitchen
10. Marché aux Puces St Ouen (p.37)
11. Formule 1 hotel (p.13)
12. Parisian Days (p.14)
13. Cook'n with Class (p.46)
14. Super Naturelle (p.46)

- 100% vegetarian
- restaurant/cafe
- shop
- hotel/ hostel
- cookery school/caterer
- local group/organisation

Au Grain de Folie
Vegetarian French restaurant

📞 24 Rue Lavieuville
Cross street: Trois Frères

☎ 01 42 58 15 57

⊖ Métro: Abbesses

🕐 M–Su 13.00–15.00, 19.00–23.00

On the tourist trail leading up to Montmartre, you'll discover this tiny little vegetarian spot that's been serving the neighborhood since 1981.

Whether you come for lunch or dinner, the formule is the same price—€13. Simple, generous composed plates of fresh vegetables—grated carrot, beet, cabbage, lettuce—share space with lentil salad, grains, and those über-popular open-faced sandwiches called tartines. Tarts, seitan stews, and other savory surprises are other possibilities. Gluten-free plates can be made on request.

The à la carte menu includes soup, vegan tzatziki, vegan pâté, and hummus (€.50 each).

Organic beer (€4.00–6.50), wines by the bottle or glass, and juices available.

Marie-Cecile, the friendly English-speaking proprietor, is sometimes the only one holding down the fort, so be patient if the service runs a bit slow. The location is ideal and the overall vibe is quintessential bohemian Paris. Snag one of the few outdoor seats if it's a sunny day and enjoy the neighborhood views. Cash only.

Bob's Bake Shop
Vegetarian and fish American cafe

📞 12 esplanade Nathalie Sarraute, opposite 39 rue Pajol
Cross street: blvd de la Chapelle

☎ 09 84 46 25 26

⊖ Métro: Marx Dormoy, La Chapelle

🕐 M–Su 08.00–16.00

🔗 www.bobsfoodetc.com
www.facebook.com/bobsfoodetc

In June 2014, the folks behind popular vegetarian spots Bob's Juice Bar (10th) and Bob's Kitchen (3rd) opened Bake Shop, a new spot not far from Gare du Nord at 22 bis rue Pajol.

"There are homemade bagels, American pastries such as pies and cookies, high end coffee and vegan smoothies," says Bob's owner, Marc Grossman. "Unlike Bob's Juice Bar and Bob's Kitchen, Bake Shop is not vegetarian, but rather pescatarian (vegetarian + fish). There are however many vegan and vegetarian items as well as gluten-free and dairy-free pastries."

Le Cambodge
Omnivorous Asian restaurant

- ☛ 20 rue Yvonne le Tac
  Cross street: rue des Martyrs
- ☎ 01 42 54 44 24
- ⊖ Métro: Abbesses
- ◕ M–Sa 12.00–22.00; Su closed

A stone's throw from the charming Place des Abbesses and its much-photographed Art Nouveau Métro station is this hole-in-the-wall southeast Asian place that makes a mean bo bun (€8.50), with crispy spring rolls atop rice noodles and just the right amount of sauce and vegetables.

Lim, the on-site owner, has seen demand for vegetarian items grow and is working to develop the veg menu. Other veg dishes are well priced and balanced in flavor, including the sautéed noodles with vegetables (€8.90) and the steamed rice with vegetables (€7.90).

You can also pop in for a simple snack like fried nem (eggless egg rolls), which come three to an order and are served with lettuce leaves and a dipping sauce for the rockbottom price of €3.20. Fresh spring rolls with noodles and vegetable are €3.20 each, and vegetable samosas are €2.30 each.

Cambodian beer (€3.60), juice, wine, and sparkling water will help keep thirst at bay.

Terrace seating. Dog-friendly. Credit cards accepted.

Gang Seng
Ominvorous Tibetan

- ☛ 40 rue Lepic
  Cross street: rue des Abbesses
- ☎ 01 46 06 71 91
- ⊖ Métro: Blanche or Abbesses
- ◕ Tu 19.00–23.00; W–Su 12.00–14.00 and 19.00–23.00; M closed

Friendly service and authentic Tibetan flavor in each plate is what you can expect at Gang Seng.

Take a seat in the tiny upstairs dining room or out on the sidewalk terrace, order a beer (€3.50–4.50), then a starter of steamed Tibetan bread (€2.50), momo (€5), or vegetable noodle soup (€9).

Mains include noodles with black mushoorm (€12), tofu with vegetables, or Tibetan fried noodles (€12).

Wine by the bottle or glass, tea, and other drinks available.

Terrace seating. Credit cards accepted.

Hope Café
Omnivorous fusion cafe

🖝 64 rue Lamarck
Cross street rue Coulaincourt

📞 01 46 06 54 40

⊖ Métro: Lamarck-Coulaincourt

🕑 Tu-Sa 10.00-24.00 (last orders
23.00), Su brunch 10.00-16.00
(except school holidays, see
Facebook), M closed

➤ www.hope-café.com
Facebook Hope café

An eclectic, organic cafe on the quiet,
less touristy north side of Montmartre
with a menu that covers every
possible food craving you might have,
from sushi to vegan burgers. The
owners are French but have done a
lot of traveling and wanted their
restaurant to reflect the culinary
diversity of their experiences.

Soymilk smoothies (€4/5/7) can be
made with or without maca and
guarana. Fresh juices (€4/5/7) are
made with your choice of seasonal
vegetables and fruits. They even offer
mojitos with organic rhum (€8.50).

Entrées include salads (€7), soups (€7)
like coconut-curry lentil, and nems
(€6) with vegetables. Vegan burgers
(€15), maki (€13) and vegetable tart
(€12) are other possibilities.

The vibe is friendly and welcoming,
and very laid-back in a California
beach town kind of way. A great spot
to spend a Sunday morning relaxing,
eating, and enjoying Paris café
culture.

Kid-friendly. Terrace seating.
Dog-friendly. Credit cards accepted.

Moulin Rouge
French omnivorous

🖝 82 blvd de Clichy
Cross street: rue Lepic

📞 01 53 09 82 82

⊖ Métro: Blanche

➤ www.moulinrouge.fr

it's the last place you'd expect to find
a plant-based meal, but the celebrated cabaret wants your business!
With both vegan (végétalien)and
vegetarian (végétarien) options, no
one has to be left out of the cancan
party. Besides a seat at the world-
famous show (the current production
is "Féerie"), the dinner-show menu
(€185) includes a demi-bottle of
Champagne or wine, plus three
courses including tartare de légumes,
soup, and salad as a starter; vegetable
fricassée for your main course; and
three different seasonal sorbets for
dessert. Vegetarian option includes
dairy and eggs.

Everyone from Elton John to Salvador
Dali and Elvis Presley have taken in a
show here, and now vegans can too.
Whoopee!

Credit cards accepted.

Le Pain Quotidien (18th)
Omivorous healthy

- ☛ 31 rue Lepic
  Cross street: rue des Abbesses
- ☏ 01 46 06 79 98
- ⊖ Métro: Blanche or Abbesses
- ◑ M–Su 08.00–22.00
- ☚ www.lepainquotidien.com

One of the Belgian chain's newest locations is in prime tourist territory, much to the joy of visiting vegetarians.

Non-meat items like the veg pot au feu with quinoa and harissa (€9.50) are plentiful and clearly marked, and most dishes come with the trademark pain (bread) served with a variety of jams and spreads. Tartines (open-faced sandwiches) change regularly; a daily special might be avocado with green beans and hummus (€9.60) with a side salad. Soups (€4.90–6.90) are often vegan and always vegetarian.

Salads are filling, if a little on the expensive side. The Detox salad with quinoa and vegetables will set you back €11.70, and the artichoke with arugula costs €13.60.

Organic wine served, as well as juice, coffee, and tea.

Kid-friendly. Terrace seating. Free wifi. Credit cards accepted.

Soul Kitchen
Omnivorous organic

- 33 rue Lamarck
  Cross street: Coulaincourt
- 01 71 37 99 95
- Métro: Lamarck-Coulaincourt
- Tu, Th-F 08.30-19.00; W 9.00-19.00; Sa-Su 10.00-19.00; M closed. Closed August
- www.soulkitchenparis.fr

The photo of Soul Kitchen's daily chalkboard menu is uploaded to their website each day, but it doesn't tell you about the homemade granola with soymilk or the daily scones, muffins, and madeleines.

Order your daily special (€12.50) at the counter and one of the nice staff will deliver it to your indoor table or seat outside in the sun. Salads are fresh and full of greens, seeds, and seasonal vegetables.

Not everything can be veganized, but ask anyway. The Tijuana Stop bowl is loaded with salsa, guacamole, brown rice, and greens, with optional crème fraiche. The Acapulco Wrap features grilled veggies in a grilled tortilla and chipotle sauce—a rare delicacy in this corner of the world.

Drinks include grapefruit juice (€3.50), iced coffee (€3.50), and wine by the glass or bottle. They charge an "alternative milk" tax of €.50, but it isn't just limited to soy, rice, and hazelnut milk; the goat milk gets it, too.

Terrace seating. Credit cards accepted.

19th Arrondissement

The 19th arrondissement straddles the Canal de l'Ourcq and is home to some of the city's most exciting music and entertainment venues. A blend of contemporary and centuries-old architecture and an intriguing mélange of cultures and cuisines—Jewish, Chinese, Arab, and African—you can't help but have a great time exploring its side streets.

Beginning in late July, Paris Plages sets up its northern outpost along the canal, and the area takes on a carnivaleseque air. The rest of the year, the banks of the canal still bustle with lively pétanque games, cyclists, promeneurs, and picnics.

Further out toward the périphérique sits the Parc de la Villette, with its museums, concert halls, children's play zones, and grassy areas for lounging.

Neighborhood favorite

Café Zoïde
Vegetarian family café

- ☛ 92 bis Quai de la Loire
  Cross street: rue de Crimée
- ☎ 01 42 38 26 37
- ⊖ Métro: Laumière
- 🕐 W–Su 10.00–18.00; M–Tu closed
- ↖ www.cafzoide.asso.fr

This 100-percent veg "kids' café" is run by a non-profit association that welcomes kids, families, and childless people alike to come in and enjoy a cheap, filling meal and have some fun.

Plat du jour (€6, or €5 for association members) is a generous portion of grains and vegetables, usually vegan, and when not, there's always a vegan option. Snacks—crêpes, cake, ice cream—are €2.

Juice, tea, or coffee can be had for €1.50.

A great place to come with young kids, who'll find entertainment with games, workshops, theater, and other activities in the upstairs playroom. Programs for teens and parents are on the menu too.

Cash only.

Cheng Da To-Fou
Vegetarian tofu shop

- 141 rue de Crimée
  Cross street: ave Juan Jaurès
- 01 42 00 59 92
- Métro: Laumière or Ourcq
- M–Su 10.00–18.00

The tofu—soft, firm, fried, and five-flavors varieties—are made fresh daily at this family-run hole-in-the-wall.

Tofu is the cheapest and possibly the highest quality in town, with big bricks selling for €1.40 and the fried and flavored varieties ranging from €3.40–7 per kilo. Try the thin little cinq parfums squares; they make a great snack!

Cash only.

Café Antipode
Omnivorous café

- 55 quai de la Seine
  Cross street: rue de Crimée
- 01 42 03 39 07
- Métro: Riquet
- M–F 12-00–14.30 and 19.00–23.00; Sa–Su 12.00–16.00 and 19.00–23.00. Bar till 02.00.
- www.penicheantipode.fr

Moored along the scenic Canal de l'Ourcq is this all-in-one organic café/theater/music venue.

During the day, you can sit on the deck and enjoy a soup and salad combination, and wash it down with a cold beer, glass of wine, or any one of their 25 different fair trade, artisanal, or organic teas.

Lunch specials are cheap and filling: for €7, you can have a tartine, soup, and salad; for €10 you can have that and a tart for dessert.

Tartines on their own are €8, mostly vegetarian, and most can be veganized.

Chips and guacamole (€4), olive tapenade with spice bread (€4) and other tapas go well with the cocktails.

A great spot for a sun-splashed lunch. At night, the venue hosts theater, music, and magic performance for adults, with the occasional children's event too. Terrace seating. Credit cards accepted.

19th Arrondissement

1. Café Zoïde
2. Café Antipode
3. Baladi
4. Rosa Bonheur
5. Okay Café
6. Café Caché
7. Les Grandes Tables
8. Cheng Da To-Fou
9. Le Chapeau Melon (p.35)
10. Le Cent Quatre

- 100% vegetarian
- restaurant/cafe
- shop
- hotel/ hostel
- cookery school/caterer
- local group/organisation

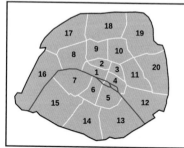

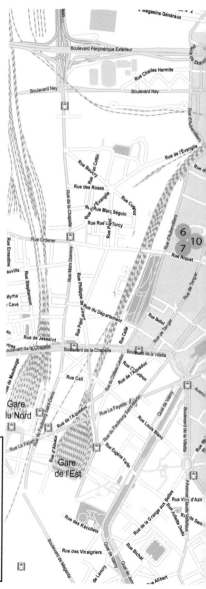

Baladi
Omnivorous Lebanese restaurant

☛ 105 rue de Meaux
Cross street: rue Cavendish
☏ 01 42 41 84 32
⊖ Métro: Laumière
🕑 M–Su 12.00–14.30 and 18.30–22.30

You'll get a warm welcome from this family-run Lebanese restaurant on a quiet street just off the canal.

Many traditional favorites—eggplant caviar (€4), falafel (€4.50), fatouche salad with fresh vegetables tossed with grilled pita bread (€5)—are inherently vegan and, not coincidentally, inherently tasty. The assiette végétarienne (€9.50) gives you the chance to try a bit of everything.

Soft drinks, wine, and that potent licorice-flavored liquor, arak, feature on the drinks menu.

Credit cards accepted

Rosa Bonheur
Omnivorous café, pub, beer garden

☛ Parc des Buttes Chaumont
2 allée de la Cascade
Cross street: rue de la Villette
☏ 01 42 00 00 45
⊖ Métro: Botzaris
🕑 W–Su 12.00–00.00, M–Tu closed
↖ www.rosabonheur.fr
facebook.com/rosabonheurparis

This beloved gay hotspot inside the picturesque Buttes Chaumont park is the place to spend a sunny summer day eating and drinking at the outdoor tables, or dancing the steamy night away inside on a hot summer (or cold winter) night.

A Spanish tapas-style menu includes olive-fig tapenade or artichoke spread and bread (€5), organic salads and wraps (€5-7), and savory cakes (€2.50).

Drinks include fresh-squeezed lemonade and juices (€4.50-6.00), beer, wine, and tea (€3.50).

A place to relax, have fun, and have a nibble while you're at it. Terrace seating. Free wifi. Credit cards accepted.

Okay Café
Omnivorous crêperie

- ☞ 41 bis quai de la Loire
  Cross street: rue de Crimée
- ☏ 01 42 01 56 04
- ⊖ Métro: Laumière
- 🕐 M-Su 12.00-23.00

The big draw at this canalside café is the terrace seating where you can enjoy a hearty buckwheat crepe stuffed with the filling of your choice, and watch the activity on the canal.

Build your own crepe (€6.60-9.10) by adding your favorite veg ingredients: Potatoes, mushrooms, ratatouille, or even pineapple, and with or without eggs or cheese. (Make sure to say "sans fromage" if you're vegan, just in case).

You can also pick something from the menu, including the market vegetable galette (€6.30), which is stuffed with seasonal vegetables. Veg soup (€5.50) and scads of salads (€8.50-10.10) ensure you won't go hungry.

Kid-friendly. Terrace. Dog-friendly. Credit cards accepted.

Le Cent-Quatre
Public cultural centre

- ☞ 5 Rue Curial
  Cross street: rue Riquet
- ☏ 01 53 35 50 00
- ⊖ Métro: Riquet
- 🕐 Tu-Su 11.00-19.00 plus
  evening shows, M closed
- ↰ www.104.fr/version-anglaise

Never mind that it used to be the city morgue; today, the Cent-Quatre is one of Paris's most interesting arts and entertainment venues. Come for the art exhibits, shops, and live performances spanning the spectrum from music to dance and theater. On weekends, the communal spaces fill with hip-hop dancers who put on a

great show for anyone who passes.

These two cafés housed inside the center offer a couple of veg options each.

Café Caché
🕐 Tu–Th 9.00–19.30, F–Sa 9.00–22.00, Su 11.00–20.00, M closed

A black and white photo booth sits just outside this "hidden café"; inside, you'll find lots of tasty beverages—wine, coffee, tea, mixed cocktails—a pleasant terrace, and a few veg options including salads, frites, and even a meatless croque monsieur.

Les Grandes Tables
🕐 Tu–F 12.00–19.00, Sa–Su 11.00–19.00, M closed

Soups, salads, pastas, and tarts are some of the things you'll find on the daily menu at this indoor–outdoor café with, as its name suggests, very big tables. Friendly staff and prime views on the dancers practicing their enviable hip-hop moves.

20th Arrondissement

There are several good reasons to venture out into Paris's easternmost arrondissement, Père Lachaise cemetery being one of the best. The pretty old graveyard—the city's largest—is the final resting place of everyone from Edith Piaf and Oscar Wilde to Jim Morrison and Gertrude Stein.

photo Roger C. Lakhani

You'll also discover some popular music and entertainment venues here, including the Flèche d'Or, which has been converted from an old train station into a hot music spot where you can catch independent bands from around the world.

If you dare, the funky Porte de Montreuil flea market can be found out here, and is one of the best spots to rummage through piles of old clothes looking for that perfect wearable treasure.

Next to the market sits a cluster of Accor hotels with rooms offering predictable comfort and cleanliness for low prices.

Neighborhood favorite

Namo Bio
Vegetarian natural foods store

- 15 rue de la Reunion
  Cross street: rue des Pyrénées
- 01 43 56 00 08
- Métro: Buzenval or Maraichers
- M–Sa 10.00–21.00, Su 9.00–12.45
- www.namobio.fr

This independent organic market is completely vegetarian and offers a good selection of readymade foods, plus breads, fake meats, bulk-bin items, non-dairy yogurts, and fresh produce (below).

Come in and stock up for a picnic in the park or a gourmet vegan dinner *chez vous*.

Credit cards accepted.

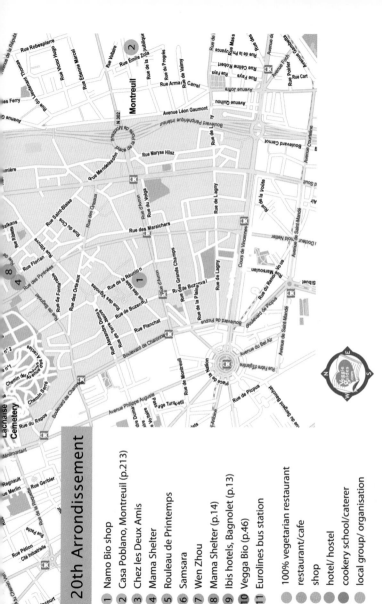

20th Arrondissement

1. Namo Bio shop
2. Casa Poblano, Montreuil (p.213)
3. Chez les Deux Amis
4. Mama Shelter
5. Rouleau de Printemps
6. Samsara
7. Wen Zhou
8. Mama Shelter (p.14)
9. Ibis hotels, Bagnolet (p.13)
10. Vegga Bio (p.46)
11. Eurolines bus station

● 100% vegetarian restaurant
● restaurant/cafe
● shop
● hotel/ hostel
● cookery school/caterer
● local group/ organisation

Restaurant Chez les Deux Amis
Omivorous Mediterranean

- 📍 110 rue de Menilmontant
  Cross street: rue des Pyrénées
- ☎ 01 47 97 04 59
- ⊖ Métro: Gambetta or Saint-Fargeau
- 🕐 M-Su 11.00-00.00

Friendly, super casual, and cheap, this little spot is the ideal stopover before a show at nearby music venues La Bellevilloise or La Maroquinerie (where there's a vegan burger on the menu, FYI). Expect simple, middle-eastern inspired tapas like hummus (€4), Mediterranean salads (€7.50), eggplant caviar (€4) and plenty of bread to mop it all up with.

Terrace seating. Credit cards accepted.

Mama Shelter
Omnivorous pizzeria

- 📍 109 rue de Bagnolet
  Cross street: rue des Pyrénées
- ☎ 01 43 48 45 45
- ⊖ Métro: Gambetta or Maraichers
- 🕐 M-Su 12.00-01.30
- ↖ www.mamashelter.com

The city's hippest hotel (pg.14) is attached to the city's hippest pizzeria, and you'll find them both out in the hinterlands of eastern Paris in an area that's become a popular nightlife destination.

Most of the entrées, such as vegetable confit (€6) or gazpacho (€6), are already vegetarian, and all the pizzas can be veganized. The Vegetarian (€13) is already cheese-free; the Vesuviana (€15) comes with or without parmesan, and includes arugula, olives, artichokes, mushroom, and tomato.

Wines are all delicious (€6 by the glass, €24 by the bottle), and soft drinks and fizzy water are available for teetotalers.

Credit cards accepted .

Rouleau de Printemps
Omnivorous Vietnamese

- 📍 42 rue de Tourtille
  Cross street: rue de Belleville
- ☎ 01 46 36 98 95
- ⊖ Métro: Belleville
- 🕐 Su-Tu 11.30-15.00, 19.00-23.00; W closed

This cheap, tasty, and tiny canteen offers a good selection of vegetarian items (€1.90-7.00) including that global favorite, bo bun (€5.80-7.00), plus a super noodley won ton soup (€5.90), the eponymous spring rolls (€2.70), and decadent, greasy boulettes stuffed with black mushrooms and cabbage (€5).

Beer, wine, and the cheapest tea in town (€.30).

Expect communal tables, Parisian hipsters, and a wait on weekends.

Credit cards accepted

Samsara
Omnivorous South Asian

☛ 3 rue du Jourdain
  cross street: rue de Belleville

☏ 01 43 66 02 65

⊖ Métro: Jourdain

🕔 M–Sa 12.00–14.30 and 19.00–
  23.30, Su closed

🔗 www.lesamsara.com/

Stellar service, kitschy décor, and balanced flavors dominate at this cozy spot not far from the must-visit Buttes Chaumont park.

Entrées include dal (€4.50), pakora (€4), and samosa (€4.50), and breads run the gamut from naan to chapatti. Veg biryani (€11) curried spinach or eggplant (€8/8.50), and pea-and-potato curry (€7) are tasty and filling.

For dessert, try the rose sorbet (€4).

Multi-course lunch and dinner menus available.

Full bar. Terrace seating. Credit cards accepted.

Wen Zhou
Omnivorous Chinese restaurant

☛ 24 rue de Belleville
  Cross street: blvd de Belleville

☏ 01 46 36 56 33

⊖ Métro: Belleville

🕔 F–W 10.30–22.30; Th closed

The lengthy vegetarian menu is a welcome sight at this popular, no-frills Chinese restaurant in the thick of Belleville.

House-made fried dumplings (€5.90), hand-pulled noodle soup (€5.50), taro with sautéed greens (€6.90), and noodles with garlic and black vinegar (€5.90) are just a few of the standouts.

Tsing Tao beer, soft drinks, tea, and wine served, plus greasy red-bean sesame balls for dessert.

Can get noisy when crowded, but it's always a good place to get stuffed on the cheap. Cash only.

Get Out of Town

You've seen the Eiffel Tower, Sacre Coeur, and the Seine, and now you're ready to venture out and see what lies beyond la périphérique. So, what is there to do and see out there? Plenty! From vegetarian B&Bs to Europe's largest Buddhist temple, there's something for everyone. Take a seat on a regional train (or a high-speed TGV) and make a day trip to one of these fun, food-oriented destinations, most of which are within three hours of Paris.

French telephone numbers are 8 digits, prefixed with:

01 Île de France (Paris and surrounding area)

02 North West

03 North East

04 South East

05 South West

96, 07 Mobile numbers

When dialling from abroad drop the 0 and use the country code 33.

When in France dialling from a landline, just dial the last 8 digits if you're in that area.

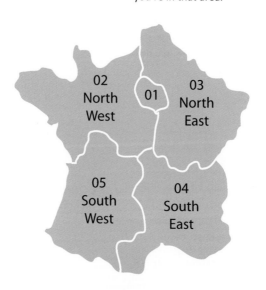

Around Paris

Île-de-France Region

Casa Poblano
Vegetarian restaurant

- 15 Rue Lavoisier, 93100 Montreuill (Seine-St-Denis)
  Cross street: rue Émile Zola
- Métro: Robespierre
- M, W-Th-F 10.00-15.00
  Tu, Sa 15.00-23.30
- www.casa-poblano.fr

This under-the-radar cultural center and collective hosts music and theater events, art expos, and weekly dining events including the popular bio gastronomique nights (gourmet organic) that just happen to be vegetarian (with a vegan option). The multi-course, pay-what-you-want meals include such tempting dishes as Gaspacho de betterave au vinaigre balsamique truffé (beet gazpacho with truffled balsamic vinegar). Tajine de légumes (black rice served with a mélange of vegetables in a coconut sauce) and chocoloate-pear-banana tart for dessert.

Organic wine (€2.50), beer (€2.30–5), fairtrade tea €1.50) and coffee (€1.30) are available at the bar.

Fo Guang Shan Temple
Vegetarian restaurant in temple

- 3 allée Madame de Montespan, 77600 Bussy Saint Georges (Seine-et-Marne)
- 01 60 21 36 36
- RER Bussy Saint Georges (two stops before Euro Disney)
- Tu-Su 10.00-17.00
- www.fr.ibps.fr

Europe's largest Buddhist temple sits just 25 miles east of Paris (and a 30-minute train ride on the RER A from Gare de Lyon) in Bussy Saint George, and every Sunday morning after the 10 am prayer service, pious guests are invited to partake in a Taiwanese vegan meal with their fellow worshippers. The price varies from week to week, depending on the menu. An on-site vegetarian restaurant is slated to open in 2014.

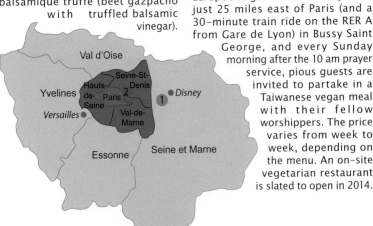

North East

Burgundy

Les Battées
Vegetarian bed & breakfast

☛ Val and Roy Patchett, Les Battées, 71510 Dennevy (Saône et Loire)

☎ 03 85 45 47 09

www.lesbattees.com
lesbatees@wanadoo.fr

Three hours and a world away from Paris sits this vegetarian B&B on a former winegrowing estate. Pleasant gardens, evening meals on request (vegan if requested), and homemade jam made from fruit grown on the premises. Vegans and those allergic to bee stings should be aware that the hosts keep bees and serve their honey at mealtimes.

Alsace

Maison Ganesh
Vegetarian holistic retreat center

☛ 14 rue du Sperberbaecher, 67140 Le Hohwald (Bas-Rhin)

☎ 03 88 08 34 57

www.terredecristal.com

Come for one of the themed weekend retreats with a holistic health focus, or just for a relaxing getaway in a woodsy wonderland in eastern France. Look for organic vegetarian meals, nature walks, and friendly hosts. No TV!

North West

Loire Valley

La Cucina di Terresa
Loire Valley Wine Tours

   www.lacucinaditerresa.com
   lacucinaditerresa@gmail.com

Besides cooking classes, market tours, and private table d'hôtes dinners, Terresa Murphy of La Cucina di Terresa (pg.34, 44, 144) offers one-of-a-kind natural wine tours in the Loire Valley, just an hour and a half from Paris. Prices and dates vary; contact for details.

Sivananda Yoga Center
Vegetarian yoga center

☛ 26 Impasse du Bignon, 45170 Neuville aux Bois (Loiret)
☏ 02 38 91 88 82
   www.sivananda.org/orleans

If you've always wanted to try a yoga retreat but didn't know where to start, this peaceful retreat in the heart of the Loire Valley is a great place to begin. Meals are ayurvedic vegetarian, and cigarettes, alcohol, and non-veg food are verboten. Choose to stay in a tent (€48-300 for 7 nights) or a single private room (€100 per night or €630 for 7 nights) and a variety of choices in between.

Also yoga and cookery in Paris. (pg. 35, 44)

Normandy

La Maison du Vert
Vegetarian hotel & restaurant

☛ 61120 Ticheville, Vimoutiers (Orne)
☏ 02 33 36 95 84
   www.maisonduvert.com

Bicycle rides, walks in the garden, and just sitting around relaxing are the top activities at this home-away-from-home in northwestern France. Vegan meals on request, organic wines, and within easy reach (an hour's drive) of tourist sites like Mont Saint Michel, D-Day beaches, and Honfleur.

South East

Languedoc–Roussillon

Le Mas Perdu
Vegetarian accommodation

🛏 Boujac, 30380 Saint-Christol les Alès (Gard)

☎ 04 66 60 76 80

🔗 www.lemasperdu.com

Relax on an organic farm in the beautiful Cevennes mountains, surrounded by lakes, rivers, fruit trees, and pleasant breezes. Meals are always vegetarian (with a vegan option), and special programs with a wellness focus are available year-round.

Provence

Maison de Josephine
Vegetarian bed & breakfast

🛏 Hameau de l'Eglise, 05600 Risoul (Hautes-Alpes)

☎ 04 92 45 28 01

🔗 www.maisonjosephine.com
maisonjosephine@yahoo.fr

Sauna, swimming pool, and great views of the Alps await at this kid-friendly, vegetarian B&B. Nearby you'll find ski resorts, excellent hiking trails, and adorable villages. A spacious communal room is available for yoga, group classes, and other events.

Rhône-Alpes

Yoga with Altitude
Vegetarian yoga retreat

🛏 winter: 1 Le Haut des Brévières, 73320 Tignes (Savoie)

summer: Mournet, 07190 Albon d'Ardèche (Ardèche)

☎ 06 03 10 65 93

🔗 www.yoga-with-altitude.net
info@yoga-with-altitude.net

Charlotte Saint Jean leads yoga retreats in the foothills of the Alps, teaches monthly classes in Paris, and offers getaways that meld vegetarian ayurvedic cooking with yoga throughout the year. English speaking instruction and different levels welcome.

South West

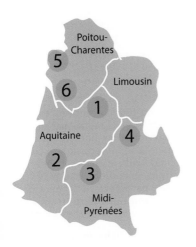

cooking is one of her many passions. B&B for two €80. Packed lunches, dinner on request.

Eco Gîte de Payan
Vegetarian self-catering

- 40630 Luglon (Landes)
- (05 58 08 32 23
- Open mid March to end November
- www.ecogitedepayan.com

A peaceful vegetarian gîte tucked in a forest south of Bordeaux, ideal for group retreats. Kitchen facilities, beautiful gardens, and a vegetarian dining policy, plus yoga and massage on request.

Midi-Pyrénées

Le Piot
Vegetarian guest house and restaurant plus omnivorous gite

- Chemin de Piot, 32500 Fleurance (Gers)
- (05 81 67 03 17
- Facebook Le Piot, Fleurance lepiot@outlook.com

British couple Danny Wright and Kerry Maloney-Wright have renovated this stately 1914 home, transforming it into a vegetarian maison d'hôtes featuring four comfy guest rooms. In summer, the swimming pool provides

Aquitaine

Auberge de Bouyssour
Vegan bed & breakfast

- Lieu-dit Bouyssour, 24750 Marseneix (Dordogne)
- (05 53 46 67 32 landline 06 88 59 51 47 mobile
- www.auberge-de-bouyssour. com
  info@auberge-de-bouyssour. com

This vegan B&B in the beautiful Dordogne Valley offers a true escape from it all. Expect to disconnect (no TV or wifi), and to be surrounded by peaceful gardens in an area brimming with castles, rivers, and rolling green countryside. Proprietor Reija Feldmann is also the chef, and vegan

cooling respite, and bicycle rentals can be arranged for local excursions.

Meals have a Mediterranean flavor inspired by food writer du jour Yotam Ottolenghi, and focus on in-season, local ingredients. A vegan menu might begin with grilled vegetable soup or roast red pepper salad, followed by chickpeas and spinach in a spicy tomato sauce served with

brown rice, or a vegetable paella. Desserts celebrate seasonal fruit, and could include a pear crumble or apples baked in Armagnac.

A night's stay will set two of you back €65–€95, depending on the room, including breakfast. For €20 more, you get a three-course dinner with wine and coffee.

Le Jardin de Cabrerets
90% vegetarian restaurant, tea room & apartments

- Le Bourg, 46300 Cabrerets (Lot)
- 05 65 22 90 75
- Easter–end Sept 2014 M–Su 11.00–23.00
- www.lejardindecabrerets.com
  info@lejardindecabrerets.com

While not 100-percent veg, this pet-friendly inn and restaurant run by a pair of longtime herbivores offers vegan- and vegetarian-exclusive holidays with a variety of boarding options, including B&B (€199 per person per week), half-board (from €285), and full-board (from €370) which includes three meals a day.

Vegan menu items include rice balls and vegetables in Thai coconut sauce; roasted red pepper, tomato, and basil soup; and mushroom pâté on toasted fig bread with chutney. Oh, yes: And crêpes with homemade dairy-free Nutella.

Ten percent of the proceeds from your stay support the non-profit organization started by owners Louise and James, which raises money for local animal organizations.

Poitou-Charentes

Tomlin's
Vegetarian guest house
& cookery school

📍 23 Rue Du Fief Gourmand,
   17290 Chambon (Charente-
   Maritime)

📞 05 46 35 65 42

🔗 www.tomlinsinfrance.com

Learn how to whip up mouth-watering meals like mushroom and smoked tofu kebabs with peanut butter sauce and Spring onion blinis with sweet pepper ragout at this lovely B&B/culinary academy in the sunny southwest. A three-hour train ride gets you into the bucolic countryside where a six nights stay with classes included will set you back €945. Short-term stays and day-rate classes available, too.

Le Logis des Quatre Puits
Vegetarian bed & breakfast

📍 17270 Neuvicq (Charente-
   Maritime)

📞 05 46 04 32 69

🔗 www.lesquatrepuits.com
   lesquatrepuits@me.com

North of Bordeaux and a short drive to the gorgeous Dordogne Valley, this vegetarian B&B offers a variety of accommodation, including self-catering gîtes. A party-ready yurt, salt-water swimming pool, game room, and optional evening meals are some of the fun and relaxing possibilities. Pet-friendly, and vegan meal options available by request.

Index

getarian

SCOTLAND

300 places to scoff, quaff, shop & drop veggie
all across Edinburgh, Glasgow, Aberdeenshire
Angus, Argyll, Ayrshire, Borders, Dumfries, Fife
Moray, Perth, Stirling, Highlands & the Islands

by Alex Bourke and Ronny Worsey

Vegetarian Guides

In the same series.

Ask your bookseller or visit www.veggieguides.com

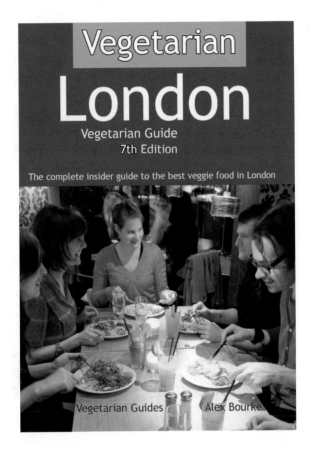

Vegetarian

London

Vegetarian Guide
7th Edition

The complete insider guide to the best veggie food in London

Vegetarian Guides   Alex Bourke

Publication autumn 2014.
Featuring 200 vegetarian restaurants & cafes
plus accommodation, shopping, social groups, maps.

For updates to this guide,
other Vegetarian Guides,
and vegan cookbooks,
visit